THE END OF CIVILIZATION

THE END OF CIVILIZATION

GORDON DONNELL

THE END OF CIVILIZATION

iUniverse books may be ordered through booksellers or by contacting:

iUniverse
1663 Liberty Drive
Bloomington, IN 47403
www.iuniverse.com
1-800-Authors (1-800-288-4677)

ISBN: 978-1-5320-0235-9 (sc)
ISBN: 978-1-5320-0236-6 (e)

Print information available on the last page.

iUniverse rev. date: 07/11/2016

INTRODUCTION

⟡

WHEN WE HEAR TODAY OF the end of civilization it usually comes as a warning of nuclear Armageddon or the impact of a hurtling asteroid. The phrase post-apocalyptic conjures up images of a morally and technologically stunted society along the lines film and fiction have conditioned us to imagine. In fact, civilization did end more than 3,000 years ago. The result was a post-apocalyptic society from which grew the western world as we know it.

In the years following 1300 BC the vast arc of land around the Eastern Mediterranean Sea was ruled by three empires; Egyptian, Hittite and Mycenaean. Within one hundred years the Hittite and Mycenaean Empires ceased to exist. Major cities across the region were destroyed or abandoned. The prevailing social order vanished. Both empires made extensive use of written language. Neither left any record of what had befallen them. The third great empire, Egypt, slipped into decay from which it never recovered. Scholars remain at a loss to explain why.

Archaeologists have painstakingly excavated the ruins of their cities for clues. Historians have learned to read the exploits of imperial rulers painted and carved on the walls of tombs and religious shrines. Diplomatic letters, bureaucratic edicts and records of merchant transactions baked into clay tablets offer a wealth of supporting detail. It has not been enough to produce concrete answers.

Written source material from any period presents difficulties. Much of it was set down in languages that no longer exist. All of it is subject to conflicting translation and interpretation. Since it served the immediate purposes of those who commissioned and prepared it, the contents are tainted by their prejudices. This can both reveal and obscure the truth. Some survives only as fragments of a larger, lost whole. Some only through reference and summary. Thus it often provides only glimpses into life and events. It cannot be read as a coherent narrative with a beginning, middle and end.

Archaeology also has limits. Only a fraction of the physical artifacts of any civilization survives thousands of years. The excavation process may produce only a random sample of those. Some known or suspected sites cannot be excavated because they lie under modern settlements. Political restrictions place others off limits. Modern conflicts make exploration in portions of the Eastern Mediterranean too dangerous. In addition, sound excavation technique requires that some material be left in the ground in context for removal in the future when better scientific tools may permit a more revealing examination.

Most of the written and physical evidence has been known for decades or longer. Egyptian hieroglyphics were deciphered in the 18th Century AD. The Hittite dictionary was essentially complete by the mid 20th Century AD. Decryption of Mycenaean Linear B followed soon after. The available material has been subjected to diligent study by scholars trained and experienced in interpreting the past. This raises the question of how it is now possible to determine the cause of the simultaneous fall of the Eastern Mediterranean empires when we do not have any significant body of new evidence. The answer is in several parts.

First, empires are distinct from the cultures that assembled them. They have their own structure and dynamics. Close study of the dominant societies will not explain the failure of empires any more than a close study of the internal combustion engine will explain traffic jams. We have to integrate knowledge of the individual Egyptian, Hittite and Mycenaean cultures with an understanding of the concept and complexities of empire.

Second, the convergence of causal events may be as important as the events themselves in determining the fate of an empire. A corollary in modern times is a strong wind blowing through a steel girder bridge. Normally this is a non-event. In one famous case, however, wind conditions were exactly right to trigger a phenomenon called aeroeslatic flutter. This is what makes a taut rope vibrate in a high wind. The span suffered a catastrophic failure, duly recorded on newsreel footage titled

Galloping Gertie. The failure was explained only when engineering analysis was expanded beyond the standard load and vector calculations.

Finally, the sporadic nature of the available evidence has sometimes worked against a solution to what caused the failure of the Eastern Mediterranean empires. Faced with an absence of information, well intentioned scholars often resorted to best guesses in an attempt to construct a comprehensive history. Unfortunately some of these guesses, consecrated by time and hallowed by usage, have become enshrined as fact. Accordingly, we will pay special attention to what we know, or think we know, and how we came to know it.

Our examination will begin with a review of the methods of source analysis, so we can understand and evaluate the material that has come down to us. This will be followed by a thumbnail sketch of the three empires under consideration, so we will have a general concept of the Eastern Mediterranean world of the time. From there we will proceed to a discussion of how ancient empires were created and the conditions under which they flourished. In order to determine how empires disintegrate, it is necessary to understand the principles on which they are built and maintained.

We will then be in a position to trace the sequence and chronology of events that brought about the overall disintegration of civilization in the Eastern Mediterranean.

Redmond, Washington
2016

LOOKING BACK IN TIME

SOME YEARS AGO A WORK crew made a gruesome discovery in a remote area of Washington State; a human skeleton. The authorities began an investigation. Missing persons records were checked. The remains were forwarded for pathology to determine whether the cause of death was natural, accidental or homicide. The mystery was finally solved after considerable scientific effort. The remains were the now famous *Kennewick Man*, who perished 9,000 years ago.

Items pulled from the ground seldom advertise their age. Fortunately the nature of the physical universe and the habits of humankind permit us to apply science and ingenuity to establish dates in the distant past. Before we journey back more than 3,000 years to the Late Bronze Age we should understand the methods used to determine the dates we will visit.

Stratigraphy

This technique is based on the fact that gravity brings everything to ground on a more or less immediate basis. A spectacular example occurred sixty five million years ago. A massive asteroid struck Mexico's Yucatan Peninsula. The force of impact sent its component elements high into the atmosphere, to be carried broadcast on air currents until they settled out. We know of the impact because the crater has been identified. We can date it because a world-wide layer of traces of the element lithium, which is more common in asteroids than on earth, settled above rock layers dated to that time. This layer became part of the world's geologic time line as layers were set down on top of it.

The date roughly coincides with the disappearance of the world's dinosaur population, leading to the theory that the impact accelerated a seismic event which was responsible for the extinction. This brings us to an important distinction. The dating is scientific, in the sense that it can be validated by repeated observation. The extinction theory is an extrapolation that may be suggested, but is not proven, by the dating.

Stratigraphy has been applied in many archaeological sites in the Eastern Mediterranean. One example is the city of Troy, which we will visit in later chapters. Troy is not one city, but a number of successive cities, each one built on the ruins of its predecessor. Occupation of the site of Troy goes back to what is referred to as the Neolithic Age, famously defined in the film *Raiders of the Lost Ark* as "Neo, meaning new, lithic, meaning stone".

A brief discussion of the concept of *Ages* is in order. Scholars have fallen into the habit of classifying human history according to the tools in common usage at various times. Stone, Copper, Bronze and Iron are the broad categories. Contrary to the timelines often published in history texts, there is no definite beginning or end to these Ages. For example, the popularly named *Iceman*, a complete set of human remains found frozen in the Alps and dated to just before 3,000 BC, was carrying both an axe with a copper blade and a knife with a stone (obsidian) blade.

The empires we will examine are dated to what is known for convenience as the Late Bronze Age, and came to grief in the 12th Century BC. Iron was being extracted in the area as early as 1,800 BC. A dagger with an iron blade was found in the tomb of the Egyptian Pharaoh Tutankhamen, who died around 1,330 BC. However it was the 9th Century BC before iron artifacts commonly outnumber bronze artifacts in archaeological excavations in the area.

While the concept of Ages is fluid, the process of stratigraphy can produce definite results. Successive strata can be dated by reference to the objects found there. Anything revealed by excavation can then be assigned a corresponding date range. The strength of dating by stratification is that it can be validated by observation and replication. Observation means that an object can be seen and/or photographed in context. Photography is important because camera media can record spectra, such as infrared, that the human eye cannot. Replication means that dating of reference samples can be repeated as many times as desired with similar results.

The primary weakness of this method, when it can be applied, is imprecision. The date of any stratum is only as precise as the dates of samples from the stratum. Those may be incomplete and subject to interpretation. Stratigraphy can be applied only when clear strata exist. This is not always the case. Items from different eras and cultures may be found in a jumbled array.

When stratigraphy is possible and properly applied we can have confidence in the results, within the limits of precision imposed by prevailing conditions.

Seriation

The dating technique of seriation is based on the transitory nature of mankind's fascination with styles. A modern example is the American automobile. Initially it resembled the horse-drawn vehicles that preceded it. As engines grew, so did hoods. The 1930s brought streamlining. The 1950s brought fins. The 1970s brought outsized bumpers. An archaeologist of the future excavating in rural America will be able to date a town by the styles of wrecked autos left behind.

Archaeologists of today rely heavily on styles of pottery to establish dates. Pottery has been basic to civilization since man first learned to fire clay. It provided durable, contamination-free storage for food and liquids, as well as the plates, bowls and drinking cups from which to conveniently consume his meals. While it can be broken, it does not decay. Archaeologists are all but guaranteed some supply, however fragmentary, at any sizeable excavation.

Fragments of pottery can be reassembled and the surface decoration either discerned visually or raised by chemical or other means. Archaeologists can then compare the piece to a reference library and determine when it was in use. In general, a popular style starts with a small following, grows to domination, and then withers to a small following as new styles come into vogue. This trend is remarkably consistent. A relative count of styles can fine-tune the dating of a site.

Seriation is the most common type of dating currently in use. Dig teams spend prodigious amounts of time recovering bits of pottery, painstakingly referencing horizontal and vertical positions in the site and then sorting and attempting to assemble the bits into recognizable objects. Photographs of the finished products are often circulated among experts to ensure correct interpretation.

Computer software now allows virtual reconstruction of pottery based on the curvature of a relatively small number of fragments. Data point mapping allows virtual site reconstruction with precise vertical and horizontal location for all fragments unearthed during an excavation. These advances have both broadened and sharpened the application of seriation dating.

The strength of seriation lies in its broad application. It can produce date ranges where none would otherwise be available. Shortcomings do exist. The date ranges can be wide. Styles may persist longer in some areas than others. Disagreements among experts are not unknown.

One application of seriation that is not appropriate to the Late Bronze Age is dating by technique and technology. This is based on the belief that modern scholars know when certain techniques and technologies came into being. Any artifact displaying these must be from a date later than the supposedly known date of inception. The underlying belief is demonstrably flawed. For example, mortise and tenon joinery has been shown by radiocarbon dating and dendrochronology (both discussed later in this chapter) to be older than originally thought. The water screw, long thought to be a 3rd Century BC development of Archimedes, is alluded to in much earlier Mesopotamian writings.

Dendrochronology

Dendrochronology is an absolute dating method based on the pattern of annular tree rings. Trees grow at different rates each year. Dry years produce less growth. Wet years produce more. When a tree is cut down, an end-on view presents a pattern of concentric rings, each representing one year's growth and each of a unique width. This pattern of thin and thick rings, particularly when taken over a longer time period, is statistically unlikely to be repeated.

The age of a tree felled today can be determined by a count of rings. The ring patterns of wood of an unknown age can be compared with those of the known pattern and, if they match at any point, a simple count of rings will give the age of the unknown piece. By a process of successively matching older and older samples, a reference chart can be built up going back many thousand years.

Archaeologists use such reference charts to compare with patterns in wooden artifacts. The year in which the tree used to produce the artifact was felled can be precisely determined. Current reference charts extend back into the Late Bronze Age for several species of Eastern Mediterranean trees. Separate charts are required for the north, consisting of modern Turkey, Cyprus and Syria, and for the south, modern Israel and Palestine. Modern Lebanon is a transitional zone. Thus, analysis of tree rings provides not only dating of artifacts, but also gives an indication of source. Further, it supports the prevailing notion that the Late Bronze Age climate of the Eastern Mediterranean was much the same as it is today.

The strengths of dendrochronology are its precision and scientific soundness. The underlying principles are proven and the results are subject to both observation and replication. Earlier techniques of visually examining rings have been supplanted by computerized statistical analysis.

One drawback of dendrochronology lies in the low survival rate of wooden artifacts of sufficient size and composition to allow analysis. A second is that the date produced is the date the tree was felled, and does not address the life span of a structure or artifact. For example, London's Westminster Abbey is in current and very public use, even though it contains elements of wood that are centuries old.

Isotope Analysis

Isotope analysis is based on unique physical properties of elements at the sub-atomic level. The chemists' periodic table of the elements gives an atomic number for each element, representing the number of protons (positively charged particles) in the nucleus. A standard nucleus is made up of equal numbers of protons and electrically neutral particles called neutrons. In the real world trace amounts of the elements are found with nonstandard neutron counts. Each neutron count represents a separate isotope of the element. Some isotopes are inherently unstable and over time will radiate any excess neutrons to return to the stable state.

The best known form of isotope dating is carbon 14, or radiocarbon, dating. The atomic number for the element carbon is 6, with a nucleus of 6 protons and 6 neutrons for a total nuclear particle count of 12. The atom's negatively charged electrons are held in a probability cloud at various energy levels. They are not part of the nucleus.

Carbon with a nuclear particle count of 14 is produced in the upper atmosphere by cosmic rays. These are intense packets of energy capable of disrupting atomic nuclei, knocking some particles out and adding others in a giant but rare game of cosmic billiards. Carbon's neighbor on the periodic table is nitrogen, which makes up about 80% of Earth's atmosphere. Nitrogen has a standard composition of 7 protons and 7 neutrons. If a stray neutron embeds itself in a the nucleus of a nitrogen atom and knocks a proton loose in the process, the resulting 6 proton, 8 neutron configuration will be carbon (by virtue of having 6 protons) with a nuclear particle count of 14. The proportion of carbon 12 to carbon 14 in the atmosphere is constant.

Carbon-based plant and animal life participating in exchange with the atmosphere maintain a constant proportion of carbon 12 and carbon 14 in their tissues. Carbon exchange with the atmosphere ceases at death. The proportion of carbon 14 begins to deteriorate as the isotope radiates its excess neutrons and returns to the stable state of carbon 12. The carbon 14 isotope has a known half-life of 5,730 years. Half life is defined as the time an isotope requires to reduce to half its former level. This decay takes place at a constant rate. This means that the death of any carbon based life-form can be dated by determining the trace amount of carbon 14 currently present in an artifact and comparing it with the standard trace amount of carbon 14 present in living carbon-based tissue.

Radiocarbon dating has been refined and cross-calibrated into a gold standard for both historic and pre-historic dating. Changes in the atmospheric proportions of carbon 12 and carbon 14 over time required development of a correction curve to maximize the available precision. Modern isotope counts are done by mass spectroscopy. This method has been used to date some widely publicized discoveries, including the *Dead Sea Scrolls* and the previously mentioned *Iceman*.

The advantages of radiocarbon dating are the wide availability of artifacts, deriving from the fact that life on Earth is carbon based, and its proven scientific soundness. Its importance was validated in 1960 when its developer was awarded the Nobel Prize.

There are some difficulties. The method is equipment intensive and requires technical expertise to execute correctly, making it expensive. Extreme care is needed to avoid contamination of the artifact to be dated. Precision deteriorates with the age of the artifact. For example, the 2,000 year old *Dead Sea Scrolls* could be dated only to a range of 385 BC to 82 AD with just more than 80% confidence. To further complicate matters, the *Dead Sea Scrolls* are presented in several different combinations of languages and scripts, suggesting that they were not written at the same time. Radio-carbon dating must be cross-checked against other indicators.

Regression From Known Dates

Once we reach the historical period, when written records begin to appear, we have more precise tools to establish dates. Many of the dates we will use in our visit to the Late Bronze Age come from a sequential list of Egyptian rulers. The list includes the spans of their reigns from the earliest Pharaohs to later rulers whose time spans we know from other records. Given known dates, it is possible to count backward through the reigns of earlier rulers to determine when they were in power.

This is not a straightforward process. The Egyptian king list has been cobbled together from several sources, including the *Palermo Stela* (discussed later), carvings left at Abydos by Pharaoh Seti I, the *Turin King List*, which may have been written down about the time of Pharaoh Ramses II and the work of the 3rd Century BC historian Manetho. Manetho's work does not survive in original form.

The Egyptian king list has been vetted to the extent possible by comparison with other sources. It is generally accepted as accurate. We will discuss validity of other regressions as they arise.

Comparison of Independent Sources

Once we have established a sequence of dates by regression from a known starting point, we are in a position to extrapolate to dates of events cited in historical documents. An example is the method by which biblical scholars determined 1000 BC as the approximate date for the ascension of King David to power. Scripture states that five years following the death of David's successor Solomon, Jerusalem was sacked by the Egyptian Pharaoh Shishak. Egyptian records establish that the Pharaoh sacked Jerusalem in 925 BC. That would place the death of Solomon at 930 BC, and assigning forty years to his reign, would place the ascension of his predecessor, David, at around 1000 BC.

We are also in a position to extrapolate document dates based on historical events. For example, the Egyptian city of Amarna was built by the Pharaoh Akhenaten and abandoned immediately following his death. The considerable trove of correspondence recovered from the site must date to the period of his reign, which we know from the Egyptian King List.

Astronomical Reference

From time to time historical documents will reference astronomical events. The best known example is the Star of Bethlehem from Christian scripture. The Earth's revolution around the sun is fixed within a small limit of precision, so it is possible to regress star tables back in time to calculate what astronomical events would have been visible in times long past at known locations. Several attempts have been made to precisely determine the birth year of Christ based on this method. Unfortunately, several possible events occurred during the period 5 BC through 3 AD that might have been the source of the reference, as well as others outside this range.

It has been asserted that an astronomical reference in Homer's *Odyssey* places Odysseus' return to Ithaca in April of 1174 BC. This conforms to the later historian Eratosthenes' dating of the Trojan War as ending in 1184 BC, with another ten years for Odysseus' return. This sort of conformance is tantalizing but inconclusive. Any number of astronomical events might be found to support other dates.

Context must also be examined for conformance. In the case of the *Odyssey,* a character refers to the nights as the longest of the year at the season of Odysseus' return, indicating sometime in the early winter. This is also supported by narrative references to cold nights and frosty mornings.

Only clearly definable astronomical events without contradiction in context can be reliably used for dating. The most useful of these are solar eclipses. Observations of major eclipses are sometimes noted in surviving contemporary writing. If the approximate date of the writing is known, it is possible to calculate precisely when a solar eclipse would have been visible in the writer's location.

Closing Notes On Dates

Dates can be the subject of vigorous debate among scholars. Competing chronologies have emerged. The differences are more often matters of precision rather than accuracy. On those occasions where specific dates are significant, dating methodology will be discussed case by case.

The conventions BC (Before Christ) and AD (Anno Domini) are retained in favor of the religiously neutral BCE (Before Common Era) and CE (Common Era). Historical dates, at least as rendered in western writing, are reckoned from the work of a 6th century AD monk named Dionysius Exiguus. No semantic legerdemain will alter that.

Dates provided by pre-Christian sources have been converted by various authorities over time and are presented as BC equivalents. The conversions were often complicated by astronomical inconsistencies in early calendars which, compounded over thousands of years, are the source of the some of the imprecision referenced above.

VOICES FROM THE PAST

THE RULERS AND SUBJECTS OF the Late Bronze Age empires are long dead but their words and the words of those who knew them and knew of them live on in written form. Reading those words has been a notable feat of scholarship. The writing comes to us in the form of symbols that have not been used in thousands of years. A Herculean effort of code-breaking was required to decipher the symbols into recognizable language. The languages involved have either died out or been modified to a significant extent. It took seventeen years to sort out the hieroglyphic Egyptian on the *Rosetta Stone*. Decades were consumed developing a Hittite dictionary. Mycenaean Linear B was the most resistant of the three forms of imperial writing. It wasn't until the underlying language was recognized as an early form of Greek that the cipher was finally broken.

Once the symbols and language were known, the task of interpretation began. Languages are rooted in culture and tradition. Each has its own context, idioms, abbreviations and omissions. These can be as important as written words in conveying meaning. Scholars faced the daunting task of divining the intent of long vanished souls who wrote and thought in an alien language about ideas and events thousands of years removed from modern experience. Different sets of scholars arrived at different interpretations of the same text. New information required revision even where previous agreement existed.

The surviving texts are often fragmentary or narrow in scope, offering only tantalizing glimpses into significant events. To piece together a narrative of the fall of the great empires, we will need to draw from several types of written material.

Contemporary Writing

Contemporary writing at its best is original material set down at the time an historical event occurred by people with first-hand knowledge of the event. Examples are diplomatic correspondence, bureaucratic edicts, personal letters and commercial records. These tend to be narrow in scope, but can form the basis for broad inference. The information that water snake was a widely used ingredient in Sumerian pharmacology may seem trivial, but the existence of an organized system of pharmacies relying on written formulation permits us to infer the presence of a sophisticated system of medical practice.

First-hand accounts can provide insight into significant events. One Egyptian from the 16th Century BC was kind enough (or vain enough) to leave a narrative of his participation in the Hyksos expulsion on the walls of this tomb. Although the account may have followed the events it chronicled by years, the events lay within living memory at the time they were set down. This is sometimes the best we can achieve within the definition of contemporary.

To obtain the full scope of larger events, we need to expand our definition of contemporary beyond first-hand knowledge to include scribes with access to oral or written witness accounts that can be collated into a comprehensive presentation such as we see on the walls of Egyptian temples and in the tombs of Pharaohs.

Various media were used to record writing in the ancient world. In one of the most permanent forms, the walls of monumental architecture were painted or inscribed. Equally long lasting, though often more scattered, characters were inscribed on clay tablets or cylinders which were then baked into permanence. Dating of the writing is usually by stratigraphy or content.

More fragile media were papyrus, which is the inner section of a reed carefully split and spread with a binder to make sheets, and parchment, which is a scrubbed animal skin. Writing on papyrus can be dated directly by radiocarbon analysis. Since parchment can be scrubbed and re-used, dating requires a combination of radiocarbon analysis of the material and chemical analysis of the ink.

Some inscriptions also survive on pottery, although the pottery has likely not survived intact. The shards are important enough to have their own name, *ostraca*, and even in piecemeal form can provide useful bits of information. Other contemporary writing may be carved into natural rock and inscribed in metal.

An important category of contemporary writing is that which survives as part of a larger body of writing unified by time, purpose and geography. An example is the previously mentioned Amarna letters, which form a corpus of diplomatic and bureaucratic correspondence left when the city was abandoned. While individual documents may provide revealing glimpses into ancient life, a cohesive body of writing can give us insight to the internal workings of the empires and show how they interacted with each other and neighboring kingdoms.

Other troves of contemporary writing provide intimate knowledge of the flow of life in ancient times. It is important to have a finger on the pulse of normal activity. Economic, cultural and technical vitality are essential underpinnings of empire. If they falter, the bureaucratic, diplomatic and military super-structure are all in danger of collapse.

The obvious advantage of contemporary writing is that it offers an account of ancient life by the people who lived it, sometimes in the moment they lived it. This allows us to see events through the prism of their culture, but it also condemns us to their prejudices and propaganda. While contemporary writing is revealing, we need to expand our search to other sources to be sure we gain a complete picture.

Later Copies of Contemporary Writing

In some cases where the original writing has been lost, we have been fortunate enough to locate copies. Perhaps the best known example comes from Judeo-Christian Scripture. For centuries the oldest known complete version of Jewish Scripture/Christian Old Testament was a copy dated to the 10th Century AD, which made its way to Israel by shadowy means from a collection in Syria. Tradition held that this copy was identical to the original, but this could not be positively established.

A set of writings from a thousand years earlier, known today as The *Dead Sea Scrolls,* came to light. A portion of the *Dead Sea Scrolls* is a generally complete copy of Jewish Scripture, less the Book of *Esther.* Upon examination, the Jewish Scripture contained within was found to conform closely to the 10th Century AD copy in some parts, but to vary in others, particularly in *Exodus.* The prevailing theory is that the text was fluid in its earlier versions, with different sects adhering to different versions, until the work was canonized around 100 AD.

We will look at Judeo-Christian Scripture in our examination, although the original does not qualify as writing contemporary to the Bronze Age. Other writing does. The Hittite Royal Archive was copied in the 14th Century BC, giving us a look into the history of the Empire. Later copies of contemporary writing provide significant stores of material we would not otherwise have, but we are at the mercy of those commissioning the copies for decisions as to what was copied. We are also at the mercy of the copying technicians for the accuracy and completeness of the material.

The term later copies should be distinguished from modern copies. Natural erosion, pollution and tourist traffic all tend to degrade original writing. Modern copies have often been made when contemporary writing was in danger of being lost. The largest undertaking to date is a copy made of all known Egyptian hieroglyphic writing and drawings, begun in the 1920's AD. Modern restoration of contemporary writing is also included in this category. Technology has progressed to the point where it is now possible to conduct pixel level manipulation of digital images to make the worn and often illegible cuneiform on 5,000 year old tablets as clear as the day it was inscribed. Modern copies are treated as contemporary writing, since the technicians involved have no agenda beyond accurate reproduction.

Early Written History

Authorities in ancient times, often for the purpose of establishing their own legitimacy, commissioned the writing of histories. These histories may survive only as fragments, or are known only because they are referenced by later writers. In some cases they form the foundation of modern history by default. We simply have no other narrative covering a given period.

Ancient historians, even though they lived centuries or tens of centuries after the events they chronicled, had access to sources lost to modern researchers. Since the validity of those sources can only be guessed at, scholars have to look to archaeological and scientific evidence where available to establish the accuracy of early written history. Even when the source is valid, two writers looking at the same set of facts can interpret them differently. The results reflect the writers' prejudices and those of their patrons.

An example outside the scope of our examination is Tacitus' *Annals of Imperial Rome*. Tacitus wrote under the patronage of an Emperor not descended from the line beginning with Caesar Augustus. In Tacitus' writing Nero, the final Emperor of the original blood line, comes off as monstrous and clownish in order to buttress the claim of later usurpers that intolerable circumstances compelled them to seize the throne from an incompetent dynasty to preserve Rome. Even with this bias, Tacitus' work is central to modern understanding of the Roman Empire and is widely cited as authoritative. Early histories will contribute to our examination, but we will need to read them with care.

Early written history will be of particular value in looking at the inceptions of the empires we will be examining. We rely on the *Palermo Stela* for the origins of Egypt and *The Edict of Telepinus* for that of the Hittites because nothing else remains and nothing exists to contradict them.

Summary and Reference

Many of the writings lost to modern scholars were known to past scholars who considered them important enough to summarize, or at least mention, in later writings which have survived to modern times. We are often indebted to these later writings for clues as to what was important in times too distant or detached for us to view directly.

This is the source of much modern knowledge of the story of the Trojan War. Homer's *Iliad* covers only three weeks of the conflict in detail. The full history was set down in a series of works called the *Epic Cycle*, of which only fragments remain. The works were summarized in a later writing called The *Chrestomathy* of Proclus, which is also now lost. We know some of its contents because it was summarized in the prologue of a 10th Century AD copy of the *Iliad*. This copy is also incomplete, so we must supplement our knowledge with material from another Byzantine work.

A similar situation exists with the Egyptian priest/historian Manetho, whose work covers the formative period of the Empire. Although lost in all but a few fragments, it is referenced in the work of the 1st Century AD historian Josephus. The references come in the context of written arguments, so we must assume our version has been redacted to support Josephus' views.

In our examination, we will be able to draw inferences based on such works, but we will need to support the inferences with corroborating data.

Lore

Much of what happened to humankind occurred before the advent of writing, and was passed orally from generation to generation until it was set down in written language. Since the events occurred before the memory of the writer and were subject to countless generations of embellishment and editing, it is not easy to separate fact from the imagination of story-tellers. Some written lore is sufficiently wide-spread and persistent that it is difficult to discount it entirely.

An example is the story of the flood presented in the Judeo-Christian Book of *Genesis*. By itself the biblical flood could easily be dismissed as a Sunday school fable. The same story, modified to fit religious differences, also appears in the Mesopotamian *Epic of Gilgamesh* and in the Greek myth of *Djukelian*. The circumstances are the same, involving a long period of relentless rainfall, suggesting that all the stories might relate to an actual event within the collective memory of humankind.

The story came to the forefront with the discovery that the Black Sea was relatively young, created when seismic activity around 5,500 BC ruptured the shore of the Aegean and allowed masses of water to inundate the low area between what is now Turkey and Ukraine. This inrush of cold sea water striking the warm land around a lake that existed in the area would produce massive evaporation. The air would become saturated, resulting in a relentless discharge of rainfall, as described in the various flood stories. The discovery does not establish the flood as fact, but it does raise the possibility that flood lore may be something more than imagination, or exaggeration of a common phenomenon.

Our examination will look at written versions of lore in the context of known or indicated events to see what we can learn from persistent memories.

Closing Notes on Written Sources

A considerable volume of writing has survived both from and referencing the Late Bronze Age. To make our examination manageable, we will need to select only the most significant of these. There is always a danger that the selection process may prejudice the conclusion. This risk is reduced by two factors. First, ancient rulers tended to trumpet the most important of the events during their rule. If those who lived through an event thought it important, it was probably important. Second, some of the material comes to us as a large whole, recovered from cities like Amarna in Egypt, Hattusas in Turkey, Pylos in Greece and Ugarit in Canaan. A large whole produces a sample statistically more likely to represent the society under study, and its interactions with its neighbors and competitors.

Equipped with an understanding of dating methodology and written sources, we are ready to journey back to the Late Bronze Age. We will begin with a picture of the Eastern Mediterranean empires, how they came to be and what they looked like around 1300 BC, just before the process of disintegration began.

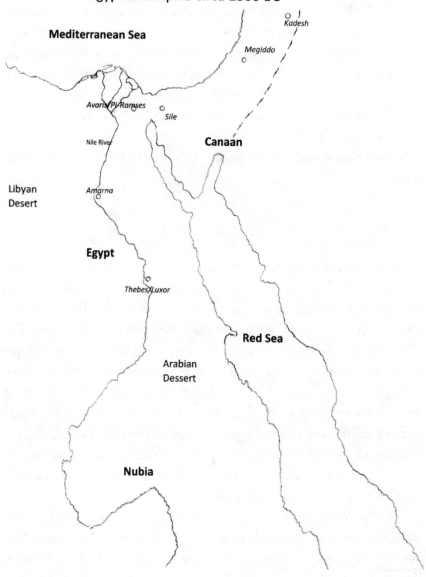

Egyptian Empire Circa 1300 BC

THE EGYPTIAN EMPIRE

O UR KNOWLEDGE OF EGYPT'S LATE Bronze Age Empire is fairly recent. When Napoleon's army arrived two hundred odd years ago, Egypt was just another destination for Muslim traders. Christians and Jews knew it as the home of biblical villains. Historians numbered it among the conquests of Alexander the Great and later the Legions of Rome. No one was aware Egypt once controlled an empire that stretched, at its maximum, twelve hundred miles from the 4th Cataract of the Nile in the south to the Euphrates River in the north.

Serious study of Egypt's past became practical with the decipherment of the tri-lingual *Rosetta Stone*, which began the process of unlocking the secret of the strange pictorial writing left behind by forgotten generations. The pictures are known today as hieroglyphs, from the Greek phrase meaning sacred symbols. While hieroglyphic writing remains notoriously difficult to read due to ancient scribes' irritating habit of omitting symbols and the need for them to adapt their work to fit the design of monumental architecture, it is our window into the Egyptian Imperial Era of the Late Bronze Age. A wealth of contemporary writing has emerged from decades of archaeological work. Organized excavation began in the nineteenth century. It continues today on a much refined basis, supported by increasingly capable technology. We now know in some detail what Egypt was like thousands of years ago.

Ruling the nation was an elite that constituted the thinnest possible veneer overlaying the substance of the population, estimated to number between two and three million in ancient times. Egypt was a subsistence agrarian economy, supported by the annual floods of the Nile. Famine was an ever-present threat that demanded the commitment of most of the population to the unending toil of agriculture. Nothing remains of the souls who struggled and perished in this environment, but they were both the beginning and the basis of Egypt. They would be the reason the nation survived when other cultures vanished.

The origin of Egypt as a nation is lost in prehistory. Settlement was in place in the Nile valley during the Neolithic age. Agricultural yield would not have been constant year to year. Crops would have been subject to pestilence. Isolated villages would have been easy prey for raiders. While no direct evidence survives, it is reasonable to postulate an evolving culture in which people were willing to sacrifice to appease gods representing forces of nature and to accept some level of central control to store food for distribution in lean times and organize mutual defense.

The earliest archeological evidence for a culture identifiable as Egyptian dates to around 4000 BC. It was excavated in an area near Luxor, well south of the Nile Delta. The Delta contained a separately ruled culture. These two were brought under single sovereignty by a historical figure known to modern scholarship as Narmer, from an English transliteration of two hieroglyphs used to represent him. The process by which his sovereignty morphed into the later dynasties of Pharaohs remains a matter of speculation.

The earliest written history of this period comes from the *Palermo Stela*, dated at around 2400 BC. Egyptian scribes of the period did not draw the same firm demarcation between physical and meta-physical that is favored by modern scholars. Many of the accounts on the *Palermo Stela* are deemed to be mythical. Fortunately, this issue and other gaps in detailed knowledge of subsequent dynasties do not bear directly on the later rise of the Egyptian Empire. The key concept to be taken from the early period is that Egyptians, and in particular the Egyptian monarchy, viewed their nation as a single entity, bounded on the South by Nubia, whose border was generally taken as the Second Cataract of the Nile, on the East by the Red Sea, on the West by the Libyan Desert, and on the North by the Mediterranean Sea.

The nation of Egypt consolidated through a succession of dynasties, but didn't achieve any geographic expansion beyond some military success in Nubia. The core of Egypt was the Nile, and its military was primarily a riverine navy. The military was probably transported and supplied by the same boats used in commerce and seldom ventured far from its lifeline. Overland expeditions were not necessary for defense. Lack of such capability probably curtailed any ambitions individual Pharaohs may have harbored. Egypt's fortunes waxed in waned during this period according to the vagaries of nature and the capabilities of the ruling elite. Paradoxically, it was the nation's most significant loss that provided it with the means for imperial expansion.

Around 1800 BC the Nile Delta came under the control of a people known as the Hyksos. This name is derived from a phrase transliterated as *Rulers of Foreign Lands.* The foreign lands are not specified. Little is known of the people. Their route to power in the Delta is open to debate. The 1st Century AD historian Josephus cited the now lost *Aegyptica* of 3rd Century BC historian Manetho as reporting a military conquest involving the looting and burning of major cities. Josephus was espousing the view that migration during the Hyksos time was the basis for events retold in the Biblical book of *Exodus*. He may have slanted his work accordingly. We do not know what sources Manetho used, what personal or cultural bias he may have had in preparing his original writings, what influence his patron, most likely the Pharaoh Ptolemy II, may have had or to what extent Manetho's remarks may later have been extracted from context. There is no archaeological evidence of widespread urban destruction during the period.

Some modern scholars have postulated a Hyksos conquest based on superior military technology, in particular the chariot and the composite bow. No report of chariot battles has survived. The idea is contradicted by at least one narrative and pictorial account placing a Pharaoh of the period in a chariot. The conveyance has four-spoke wheels and an axle placed under the center of the car, a crude precursor to the sophisticated imperial war machines with more stable six-spoke wheels and aft-placed axles that would evolve over the following centuries.

One competing scenario for the Hyksos incursion is that they were invitees; craftsmen, laborers and others brought in to work on some large project undertaken by a Pharaoh. Other sources suggest they simply drifted into the Delta over time, following the scent of opportunity. No evidence exists to establish they were of uniform ethnicity.

The proposed scenarios are not mutually exclusive. It may be that the Hyksos came to rule the Delta through some combination of invitation, migration and military action. Rule they did, however, at the expense and to the displeasure of the traditional Pharaohs. By 1600 BC Egypt was split in two and the Hyksos were solidly established in their administrative center at the Delta city of Avaris. In the years following, the Hyksos' Chief Administrator wielded sufficient power to directly challenge the traditional Pharaoh, in this case Sequenenre Tao, who ruled Upper Egypt from the city of Thebes.

Since we have reached the point in our examination when we will deal with individual players in the drama, we need to clarify how we identify them. The names follow modern scholars' convention without regard to how they might have been known in their own times. Pharaohs of the time had at least five different names, used for various purposes. Most are unwieldy. For example, the throne name of the most influential Pharaoh of the Late Bronze Age was User Maat Re Setep En Re. For convenience he is known as Ramses II. Additionally, much ancient writing was done without vowels. The vowels in the previously mentioned Narmer are modern insertions for easier reading. While the names of the players are generally agreed, spelling vagaries do exist.

Sharp force head wounds visible on the mummy of Sequenenre Tao establish that he came to a violent end, although not necessarily in battle with the Hyksos. War with the Hyksos was seen as risky and expensive by the advisers of a successor Pharaoh, Kamose. They counseled a more conciliatory approach in order to preserve lucrative business relations with the Delta.

Kamose took the traditional view that the Pharaoh was destined to rule all Egypt. He sailed north at the head of an army in the third year of his reign, laying the foundation for a fundamental change in the nature of Egypt. Based apparently on successful raids, Kamose announced total victory over the Hyksos. In fact, Kamose reign was short and he did not invest the Hyksos capital of Avaris. He was succeeded by Ahmose I. The date of succession is not precisely known, but 1560 BC is centrally located within the range established by radiocarbon dating.

Ahmose I took a more strategic approach to defeating the Hyksos. He cut the Horus Road, the main artery between the delta and Canaan, and isolated Avaris. The city fell after a protracted siege. Other cities had to be conquered one at a time. The effort required a sizeable standing army capable of withstanding the rigors of extended campaigning. It was not until around 1540 BC that Ahmose I was able to reduce the last Hyksos stronghold at Sharuhen in Gaza, completing what has come to be known as the Hyksos expulsion.

Egyptian history has its share of overstatements. The term Hyksos expulsion ranks among them. The majority of the Hyksos were professionals, merchants, craftsmen, traders, laborers and others who functioned as part of the day to day economy. They were likely integrated into Egyptian society following the destruction of a relatively small Hyksos military and political elite. The extent and mechanics of integration are subjects of speculation because the Egyptians destroyed all trace of Hyksos civilization. Part of this destruction was probably purification, scrubbing the walls of Egypt clean of Hyksos graffiti. Part was to sever any ties to the old culture felt by the newly minted Egyptians. An Egyptian identity would be essential for the coming enterprise. Conquest of Egypt's Asiatic Empire.

The Hyksos expulsion put in place the elements necessary for Egyptian expansion. The fall of Sharuhen left a large Egyptian army in Gaza where it could strike into Canaan, the modern nations of Palestine, Israel, Lebanon and Syria. Former Hyksos merchants and traders offered a network of contacts throughout Canaan from which intelligence could be gathered, sea-going ships procured and logistics arranged. On this foundation began the Egyptian Empire, which grew and fell during the period known as the New Kingdom stretching, rounded to the nearest century, from 1600 BC to 1100 BC.

Imperial conquest was not a continuous process. The Pharaoh Hatshepsut, notable as one of Egypt's few female rulers, sought to expand the nation's wealth and influence through trade rather than through empire building. The height of geographic expansion came during the campaigns of her co-regent and successor, Pharaoh Thutmose III, who ranged through what is today Southern Syria and crossed the

Euphrates River. Following the successes of Thutmose III the Empire fell into a period of decline. The Pharaoh Akhenaten focused on an ill-starred effort to convert Egypt to monotheism. The ascension of Pharaoh Seti I just before 1300 BC marked the beginning of an effort to re-conquer lost areas and re-establish the former glory of the Empire.

Egypt was not only a military and political force, but also a center of culture and learning. It had already produced the artistic tour-de-force that we view today as the grave goods of Pharaoh Tutankhamen. The *Rhind Mathematical Papyrus* displays a wide range of skills involving practical applications of algebra and geometry and calculation of area and volume, as well as reference tables. The *Ebers Papyrus* details hundreds of medicinal formulas and remedies. It also covers a range of topics from gynecology to intestinal disease to bone setting. Information on surgical procedures survives in the *Edwin Smith Papyrus*, which details treatment of trauma such as suture, bandaging, splinting, disinfection and stopping bleeding. The overall level of medical knowledge appears superior to that of Hippocrates, who lived a thousand years later and is considered the father of modern medicine.

There must have been a substantial body of computational skill and/or descriptive geometry underlying Egyptian feats of civil and mechanical engineering. The methods used to construct monuments are lost to us, but the results remain impressive. The Great Pyramid at Giza is square to within one inch over a distance of 756 feet. The orientation of the north face differs by less than $1/20^{th}$ of a degree from astronomical north. This level of precision called for skilled craftsmen. A robust trade and shipping network was required to source the appropriate materials. Construction called for a high level of technical sophistication.

The Late Bronze Age Egyptians are known to have used at least four of the six basic machines; the lever, inclined plane, wheel and axle, and wedge. Only the screw and the pulley appear to be later leaps of sophistication. The annual flooding of the Nile required a precise and extensive system of land surveying to re-establish the boundaries of farms each year. Beyond a rope soaked in water, sun dried and coated with wax to maintain length, we know nothing of the surveying tools they used to civilize the great river. We do know they had a device for computing azimuth (arc along the horizon) from the stars.

According to tradition, the first rulers of Egypt were gods. By 1300 BC one living god, the Pharaoh, presided over a complex system of governance. Below the Pharaoh were the Vizier and the High Priest of Amun. The Vizier was the chief civil administrator. The nation was divided into 42 nomes, geographic regions comparable to modern counties. Each had its own executive in charge of the local civil administration, who reported to the Vizier. The High Priest of Amun, the chief god in the Egyptian pantheon, was Egypt's ceremonial religious leader. The reality was that the cults of lesser gods competed as fiercely for converts and resources as do today's religions and sects.

The subordinate states that made up the Empire were administered differently. An Egyptian cadre was put in place to oversee administration of the conquered region. A son of the local ruler was taken to Egypt to be raised according to Egyptian customs and procedures. When his education was complete, he would be returned as the nominal ruler of his people. Evidence of Egyptian influence in wealthy Canaanite burials from the period suggests the system was effective in bringing vassal states into the Egyptian sphere.

The art, science and organization underlying the Egyptian Empire were the province of the elite, but the population at large certainly benefited from the inflow of wealth. Religious festivals provided relief from the drudgery of agriculture. Food was ample and the diet varied. Musicians and dancers performed in the public squares. Luxuries from foreign lands could be had by the fortunate and admired by the rest. In 1300 BC Egypt stood at the pinnacle of Late Bronze Age civilization, a testament to what the intellect of man could conceive and what his hands could render.

Wealthy and powerful Egypt may have been, but it was not alone in its quest for regional dominance. To the North, in Anatolia and Syria, lay the empire of the Hittites. The common border was fluid and uneasy, with cities and principalities changing hands according to the relative military power and fortunes of the abutting empires. Ambition simmered on both sides.

Hittite Empire Circa 1300 BC

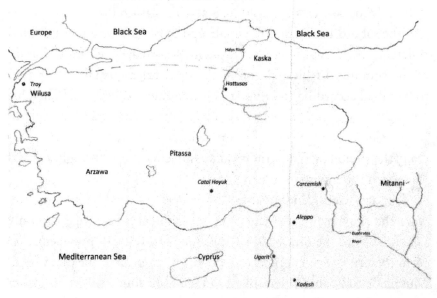

THE HITTITE EMPIRE

LESS THAN TWO HUNDRED YEARS ago, scholars either dismissed the Hittites as a Biblical fable or saw them as a minor Syrian tribe. The name Hittite comes to us from Judeo-Christian scripture. The empire builders called themselves *Rulers of the Land of Hatti*. It has never been established with certainty that the Biblical Hittites and the *Rulers of the Land of Hatti* were the same people, but the name Hittite has endured so we will use it.

Modern knowledge of the Hittite Empire began with archaeological work in the late 19th century AD. The Hittites were prolific in their production of writing. By the early 20th Century AD a vast royal archive of cuneiform tablets had been unearthed at the long abandoned imperial capitol of Hattusas. Some of this trove was in the known diplomatic language of Akkadian and could be read immediately. The rest had to wait until the Hittite language was initially sorted out over the following decades. From the archive, other writing and archaeological work we get a picture of the empire that grew out of the Anatolian region of what is now Turkey.

Anatolia is an environment much different from Egypt. There are no navigable rivers. Commerce and travel proceed overland. Much of the terrain is mountainous, rising as high as 13,000 feet and cut by steep gorges. Weather ranges from dangerously cold in the heights during winter to lowlands where a hundred degrees Fahrenheit qualifies as a cool summer day. Tarantulas and vipers still infest remote areas, although the lions hunted and stylized in stone by the Hittites are gone now. The advantage of Anatolia as a center of empire was its location. It lay at the trade crossroads of the Late Bronze Age world. To the South were Syria and Canaan and beyond them routes into North Africa. To the East was Mesopotamia and routes into the mineral rich areas of Afghanistan and ultimately India. To the North lay Europe and to the West the populous islands and coasts of the Aegean and Mediterranean Seas.

Settlement in Anatolia has been dated to the Neolithic Age. Agriculture and animal husbandry were the pillars of the economy. The earliest known of all the ancient cities was found at Catal Huyuk. By the Bronze Age, cities had proliferated. There may have been alliances among rulers, but nothing like the sense of a single nation that prevailed in Egypt. The Hittite Empire would have to be stitched together out of a patchwork of cultures.

The origin of the Hittites, who they were and where they might have come from, has traditionally been inferred from language. The Hittites wrote in an Indo-European language, meaning their writing was closer to the modern English of this book than to the ancient languages of the Near East. Based on this it has been theorized that the Hittites migrated into Anatolia from Europe. Historians are fond of migration theories. They will generally concoct several to squabble over when they cannot explain the appearance of a group of people in the written or archaeological record. Support can be tenuous. For example, the Hittites left behind an old prayer which has their Sun God rising out of the sea. Since there are no seas to the immediate west of Anatolia, One theory has them migrating in from the northwest, along the western shore of the Black Sea, another from the northeast, from the western shore of the Caspian Sea. Both may be akin to archaeologists excavating a church in the Southern United States 4,000 years from now and deducing from scraps of a Bible that the residents of Alabama migrated from Nazareth by way of Bethlehem.

The theory that the Hittites migrated into Anatolia has additional shortcomings. There is no uniquely Hittite tradition of myth and literature that might have travelled with them. The literature that has turned up includes tales of Sargon and a translation of the *Epic of Gilgamesh,* both from Mesopotamia. There is no archaeological displacement in the form of conquest or cultural shift on any of the routes along which the Hittites would have had to move during the period proposed for their migration southward into Anatolia.

The idea that the Hittites' written language indicates that they migrated into Anatolia from the north is not as solid as it might initially appear. Other Indo-European languages were in use in Anatolia at the time of the Hittite ascension. One such language, related to Hittite, is called Luwian. It was widely used, even in the Hittite capitol, but was written differently. Hittite was written in cuneiform adapted to the language. Luwian used a separate set of symbols employing more pictographs, which suggests greater antiquity. Indo-European language in Anatolia may have pre-dated the Hittites rather than arrived with them. The Hittites themselves said their language was from Nesa, an Anatolian city within their sphere. In other words, they co-opted an Indo-European language after coming to power in Anatolia.

Scholars specializing in language have conducted numerous word comparison studies to isolate the origin and map the spread of the Indo-European language group. One study raises the possibility that Anatolia was the birth-place of Indo-European. Unfortunately there is no rigorous proof. Other studies place the origin in other locations. Absent agreement, it is not possible to use language to determine the source of the Hittites.

Recent developments in genetic analysis have given us another tool to examine the origins of homogeneous groups of people. Every human cell carries DNA (deoxyribonucleic acid). Each cell contains 46 chromosomes in pairs, half inherited from the mother, half from the father. Chromosomes contain the DNA in sections called genes. The sequence of DNA in the genes is the code that tells the body which proteins to make as new cells are created to replace old ones. These proteins determine individual makeup. Each person has a unique DNA signature. Men differ from women in that they have both X and Y chromosomes, while women have pairs of X chromosomes. The Y chromosomes are passed down the male line intact, with the exception of rare mutations.

These mutations can be used to identify distinct sequences of DNA called haplogroups. Males with the same haplogroup share a common male ancestor. Haplogroups incorporate smaller sequences of Y-DNA called haplotypes. These markers of the male line allow migrations to be traced. The distribution of haplogroups and haplotypes in modern populations reflects the makeup of their male ancestry. The haplotype commonly associated with Anatolia is designated R1. Studies of the distribution of the R1 haplotype suggest migration from, rather than into, Anatolia.

We do need to be careful in accepting conclusions drawn from DNA. While the underlying science is sound, it has given rise to considerable speculation. An example can be found in Northern Ireland. Regional lore has several clans in the area claiming descent from a warrior-king named Niall of the Nine Hostages. The region's population has been found to contain a concentration of haplogroup R-M269. From this coincidence has arisen the idea that members of this haplogroup are descended from Niall. Unfortunately Niall perished in an overseas raid around 405 AD. The whereabouts of his remains are unknown. There is no physical evidence that Niall himself was a member of haplogroup R-M269.

A similar situation occurs in Asia, where a haplogroup has been attributed to Genghis Khan. The tomb of Genghis Khan remains an elusive prize of archaeology. Until the steppes of Mongolia disgorge a viable exemplar, no conclusions about the great Khan's DNA are warranted. Tracing Hittite royalty through DNA is equally problematic. Contemporary writing indicates that kings were cremated. DNA may provide signposts pointing to an Anatolian origin for the Hittites, but it offers no definite proof.

Excavation and translation continue and, coupled with emerging science, may someday answer the question of Hittite origins. For now we are left with conflicting interpretation and inference. While the Hittite writings we have recovered do not address the origin of the people, they do speak volumes about their activities.

We do not have contemporary writing from the earliest Hittites, but we do have written history in the form of the *Edict of Telepinus*. Telepinus, a later king, came to power around 1530 BC, following a period of turmoil in the Hittite royal family. Unlike the Egyptian Pharaoh, who was a living God, the Hittite king was merely a human representative of the Storm God, and was not deified himself until after death. Telepinus would, like all rulers before and since, have been eager to cement the legitimacy of his power. He may have exaggerated the issues that brought him to the kingship, but later Hittites accepted his *Edict*, and we have nothing to contradict it.

According to a copy of the *Edict* commissioned by a king who ruled a few centuries later, the Hittites established a kingdom, although not yet an empire, in the 18th Century BC. Archaeologists found the capitol city, Hattusas, ruined but essentially as the Hittites left it more than 3,000 years ago. At the peak of Imperial power the walls enclosed about 300 acres. The royal family lived in a relatively small palace area surrounded by the dwellings of their supporting nobility and business community. Carvings in the walls give us a picture of a stocky race of hook-nosed people in conical head-dress.

The location of Hattusas is fearsome, overlooking a narrow gorge along the Halys River. It is thought to have been selected for defensive potential rather than any political or religious significance. The Hittites had reason to expect trouble. They made plenty of it themselves. Early kings fought their way into Syria. Mursilis I ranged eastward and in 1595 BC sacked the city of Babylon.

Babylon was noteworthy among the ancient cities of Mesopotamia. It is recognized today as an early center for the study of mathematics and astronomy. Royal scholars were able to produce tables measuring the timing of the position of stars and planets, even down to a difficult 21 year charting of cycle of Venus. In its time the city was the capitol of a powerful kingdom. Its fall was a testament to both the military capability of the Hittites and their ability to project it over considerable distance.

The Hittites withdrew after sacking the city and Babylon fell under the control of the Kassites, a people from the mountains of what is now Iran. It has been suggested that the Hittite sack of the city was at least expedited and perhaps made possible by an alliance with the Kassites. If so, it would presage the diplomacy used in welding together the later Hittite Empire.

The extent of Mursilis I's imperial ambitions never came to be known. He was murdered on his return from Babylon and the Hittite kingdom fell into a period of disarray as homicide among the royal family became the route to power. Order was eventually restored by granting emergency authority to a governmental body outside the circle of palace intrigue. This arrangement was nothing like the parliamentary monarchies that would emerge in Europe many centuries later, but it did stabilize the internal Hittite political situation to the point where they could again focus on opportunities for conquest.

Hittite expansion grew out of a combination of military prowess and adaptability. Cities and kingdoms confronting the Hittite Imperial forces would be offered the chance to accept alliance with the Hittites. The alliance was de-facto vassalage, but the alternative was to be overthrown by force of arms. Whether the vassal states had to be conquered or simply acceded, they were allowed to maintain many of their institutions. Hittite officials overseeing vassal states often adopted local customs, which tended to reduce resistance. The Hittites maintained power through military might, but spear-point diplomacy was more palatable than no diplomacy at all.

The Hittite imperial period stretched from 1450 BC until 1200 BC. This is known as the Hittite New Kingdom, separate from the Egyptian New Kingdom. From the time of Telepinus until the New Kingdom, we have limited contemporary writing from the Hittites, although we do know of internal struggles in Western Anatolia and differences with the Syrian kingdom of Aleppo. The New Kingdom brought volumes of writing to detail the building of the Hittite Empire.

The Empire began with Anatolia as its core and expanded eastward into Northern Mesopotamia, where it encountered the powerful kingdom of Mitanni, home of the Hurrians. Pressure against the Hurrians by the previously mentioned campaigns of the Egyptian Pharaoh Thutmoses III may have assisted early eastward Hittite expansion. Hittite campaigns also ranged southward into modern Syria and Lebanon, a thrust that would eventually bring them into conflict with the Northward expansion of the Egyptians.

As with the Egyptians, the process of Empire building was not a simple linear expansion. The Hittites endured many setbacks, including palace intrigues, foreign invasions and revolts among subject peoples. At one point the capitol of Hattusas was sacked and burned. Other cities would serve as temporary headquarters until Hattusas was rebuilt in its current form.

The Empire saw its greatest expansion under the kings Suppiluliumas I and Mursilis II, who ruled during the period when Egypt's Pharaohs allotted reduced priority to expansion and defense of their empire. Numerous Egyptian vassal states in southern Syria fell during the Hittite advance. The extensive Hittite archives from this period are corroborated in key areas by Egyptian diplomatic correspondence and by contemporary writing from vassal states. By about 1300 BC the Hittite Empire's southernmost reach approximated the modern southern border of Lebanon where they confronted a resurgent Egyptian Empire.

The Hittite Empire was more than a simple accumulation of territory. Geographic location made it the keystone of the Eastern Mediterranean economic complex. It provided safe overland routes for traders and secure ports of call and provision for Mediterranean merchant fleets. Without the Hittite Empire, commerce would become exponentially riskier and more difficult. The raw material from which the Eastern Mediterranean empires were built would become scarce. The finished goods that paid for them would languish without markets.

The Hittite Empire was also more than a collection of kingdoms held in thrall simply by the application of brute force. The Empire has left a record of diplomatic activity revealing an intricate network of both internal and foreign relations used to maintain the integrity of the Empire and secure it against external forces. Documentary and archaeological evidence establish widespread and robust trade among vassal states and with sources and markets outside the Empire. The picture that emerges is of a dynamic and self-sustaining commercial and social network, not without technical and artistic achievement.

The remains of the Hittite capitol Hattusas, now a UNESCO site, stand as mute testimony to skill in civil engineering and construction. At first glance the city is remarkable for its urban planning and organization. Closer inspection reveals a brilliantly conceived and precisely built water delivery system.

Beyond works of construction and a vast royal archive, the Hittites also left massive rock carvings and stone sculpture. Many smaller works of art and craft created by the Hittites compare well with the best from contemporary Egypt, and with a more ominous Eastern Mediterranean Empire, the Mycenaeans of Greece.

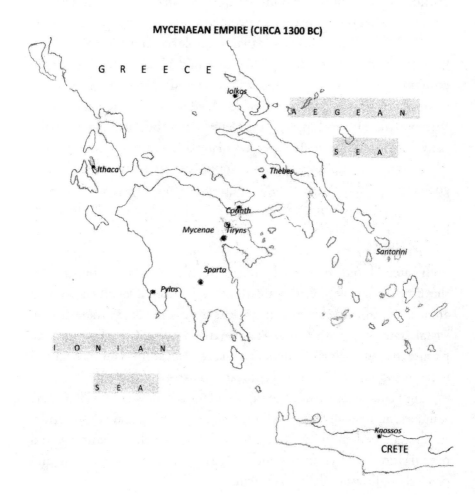

MYCENAEAN EMPIRE (CIRCA 1300 BC)

G R E E C E

Iolkos

A E G E A N

S E A

Ithaca

Thebes

Corinth

Mycenae Tiryns

Sparta

Santorini

Pylos

I O N I A N

S E A

Knossos

CRETE

THE MYCENAEAN EMPIRE

I N THE LATE 19ᵀᴴ CENTURY AD a German businessman named Heinrich Schliemann arrived in Turkey backed by a fortune made in the California gold rush. He was determined to locate the city of Troy, the setting of Homer's epic poem the *Iliad*. Scholars of the time believed that the Trojan War was myth and that Homer's work was pure theater, which is unusual in light of historical perspective. The 3ʳᵈ Century BC Greek historian Eratosthenes dated it as a real event taking place between 1194 BC and 1184 BC. Pilgrimages were made to the site by the Persian conqueror Xerxes and by Alexander the Great. The Romans claimed ancestry from the post-war Trojans, specifically a fugitive Trojan prince named Aeneas. Julius Caesar wrote of visiting the ruins of Troy in 48 BC.

Schliemann funded excavation at the mound of Hissarlik in Anatolia near the Dardanelles. The dig uncovered layer upon layer of ancient cities, including a Late Bronze Age citadel. Schliemann declared victory and decamped for mainland Greece to locate the city of King Agamemnon, leader of the Homer's Achaean invaders. A city called Mycenae, already under excavation, seemed the best choice. Absent proof to the contrary, Schliemann once again declared victory. The name Mycenaean has ever since been applied to the Late Bronze Age civilization that occupied modern Greece.

In 1952 AD the Mycenaean script, called Linear B, was deciphered. The decipherment brought some red faces to scholars of the day, who had insisted that the underlying language was not Greek. One of the key breakthroughs in decoding was the realization that Linear B represented an inflected language, in fact an early form of Greek. Linear B is unlike modern written Greek, which uses symbols to represent consonants and vowels. Its core group of symbols represents syllables. A table of core syllables is included at the end of this chapter for illustration. In addition there is a sizeable set of ancillary symbols used to represent common items such as sheep or cows, suggesting older pictographic roots for the writing. Calligraphic analysis suggests that the records of even the larger cities were kept by fewer than one hundred individuals, evidence that a class or guild of scribes existed within Mycenaean society.

The Mycenaeans recorded the daily business of commerce and administration on soft clay and recycled their tablets after use. Much of the writing we have from the Mycenaeans was preserved as the result of the burning of a coastal city called Pylos, dated at around 1180 BC. Records in soft clay were baked into permanence by the city's final conflagration, providing an uncensored snapshot of a moment in time. This preservation was a rare event, and leaves us with a picture opposite to that which we have of the other empires of the period. The history of the Egyptians and Hittites is drawn from royal or funereal archives. These give a broad perspective of the empires, rendered with the official bias of the political and social structures in which they were created.

Revealing as the Pylos preservation is, it is also narrow in scope. We are left only with everyday lists and commercial records. We have found no written history of the Mycenaean Empire, nor any contemporary documentation relating to the structure or composition of the Empire. The evidence that Mycenaean culture constituted an empire is drawn from outside sources. The archives of the Egyptian Pharaoh Thutmoses III contain reference to a ruler of mainland Greece. Included is the hieroglyph of a bird representing the syllable *wr*. This is generally transliterated to the English word *great*. It is taken be a generic reference to an overall ruler or chief, indicating that there was one authority recognized as holding power. Hittite documents from the period indicate that there was an overall Mycenaean authority on a par with the Hittite Empire, with whom they engaged in diplomatic relations. The outside sources provide no specifics as to the make-up of the Empire. We must develop our picture by inference and extrapolation from the records of a few locations, from secondary sources and from archaeology.

Greece is not a physical location conducive to empire building. The central corridor, known as the Vardar Valley, is separated from the coast by rugged mountains, as is the fertile northern plain of Thessaly. To the south lies the Peloponnese, connected to the mainland only by the narrow Isthmus of Corinth and otherwise surrounded by sea.

We have no record of what strategic importance the Mycenaeans attached to the Isthmus of Corinth, but we have clues from the behavior of later civilizations. No less a personage than the Emperor Nero was on hand to inaugurate the construction of a canal through the isthmus during Roman times. The later Emperor Vespasian committed 6,000 Judean slaves to the task. The project was never finished. Transit across the Isthmus was via a system of tracks and a machine called a *diolkos,* built in the 6th Century BC. It was still in service in the 12th Century AD. No mechanism is maintained for eighteen centuries unless the service it provides is indispensible.

Modern engineers returned in the 19th Century AD. Presumably the Roman survey was valid, since construction of the modern canal followed and destroyed the ancient works. The result was a remarkable feat, with near impossibly steep slopes of one unit horizontal for every ten vertical through ground rising in places over 250 feet, with very little reinforcement required. In World War II, the invading German forces dropped paratroops to seize the canal bridges and cut off British retreat. When the Germans in turn retreated three years later, they blew a million cubic yards of material into the canal. It was finally re-opened with considerable effort in 1948 AD.

During Mycenaean times the isthmus was controlled by the city of Corinth (*Ko-Ri-Ni-Ti* in Linear B). The geography of the Empire, sited on two land masses and numerous islands, dictated reliance on coastal and inter-island seafaring. This could be perilous. The strait between Cape Malea at the southern tip of the Peloponnese and the major island of Crete is the most treacherous water in the Eastern Mediterranean. In addition, the Aegean Sea is home to strong winds and currents. Mycenaean boats lacked keels deep enough to aid in sailing against the wind.

Absent internal lines of communication and movement to facilitate strong central control, the Mycenaean Empire appears to have formed as a confederation of city-states. How the confederation came into being is a matter of conjecture. Normally archaeologists dig down through layers of civilization to reconstruct development, since cultures tend to build on the ruins of their predecessors. However, cities like Mycenae were built on rock, so that any record of prior inhabitants was assimilated or obliterated rather than buried.

One exception is the city of Iolkos in Thessaly, the legendary home of Jason and departure point for the voyage of Argo. Digs in the area have traced pre-Mycenaean Neolithic civilization back to the 5th Millennium BC. A later Mycenaean palace and tomb have been excavated in the area. Palaces and tombs hold clues to the origins of the Mycenaeans. Speculation centers on Anatolia, based on similar application of a major architectural feature called a megaron, a large royal hall with a hearth in the center surrounded by four pillars which supported the roof, found in the palaces of both areas. Mycenaean burials in shaft graves are also similar to some Anatolian finds.

Mycenaean arrival in Greece may not have been by a direct route. Prior to the rise of the Mycenaean Empire a civilization called Minoan, after the mythical King Minos, ruled Crete and nearby islands. The Minoans were technologically advanced. Cities were served by aqueducts that fed plumbing of terra cotta pipes. Cambered roads connected key areas. The Minoan's most famous written artifact, the *Phaestos Disc*, was printed rather than produced by calligraphy; a technical leap unique for the time. What the disk says is not known, but printing suggests mass production. Printing of individual documents was not commonplace until the development of the Underwood Model 5 typewriter in 1900 AD.

Mycenaean Linear B writing appears to have evolved from a Minoan script called Linear A. Linear B was decrypted through a fortuitous combination of inspiration, brute force compilation of frequency of symbols and relation of the underlying language to Modern Greek. Scholars have not been as fortunate in their efforts to crack Linear A. Many of the symbols are similar, but the underlying language is unknown. Whatever the Minoans had to say remains unreadable. Such Mycenaean writing as we have is silent as to Minoan origins.

DNA analysis of Neolithic remains from both Crete and mainland Greece show different results. The Cretan samples show a high frequency of the haplogroup J2a-M410, associated with Anatolia. The Greek samples, from the northern areas of Thessaly and Macedonia, show a high frequency of the haplogroup J2b-M12, associated with the Balkan region of Europe. It has been suggested that the Minoan civilization of Crete established colonies on mainland Greece during the Bronze Age, marginalizing earlier Neolithic settlers as the European colonists did in North America. Minoan colonists, isolated from their own culture, may have found it convenient to adopt or modify local languages.

In the middle of the 2nd Millennium BC, Minoan civilization fell victim to a natural catastrophe. The Minoan island of Thera (modern Santorini) was devastated by a volcanic eruption. The event exceeded anything witnessed in modern times. It is thought to be the fourth most violent eruption ever, estimated by some experts as ten times more powerful than the eruption that destroyed two thirds of the Pacific Island of Krakatoa in 1883 AD. The Krakatoa eruption, heard 3,000 miles away, is reckoned as the loudest sound in recorded history. It produced a tsunami that killed 36,000 people.

The Santorini eruption triggered a tsunami that dwarfed Krakatoa. With only 60 miles to travel between Thera and the main Minoan Island of Crete, the wave would have maintained massive force. As it neared Crete the harbors and coves would have been sucked dry, magnifying the volume of the wave. Water would have come ashore within minutes, taking the path of least resistance. The height of the wave's debris field has been measured at more than 20 feet in places and is estimated to have reached beyond 50 feet in others. As shown by modern tsunami events in Aceh and Japan, this level of inundation would obliterate both the coastal population and infrastructure.

Following the tsunami would have come a more persistent and insidious threat. Winds patterns in the area are driven by prevailing high atmospheric pressure over South Central Europe. The resulting north to south flow would have spread the ash cloud from the Thera eruption over Crete where large quantities of particulate would have settled out, choking the agriculture upon which the Minoans depended. Chinese records contemporary with the Santorini eruption speak of a volcanic winter lasting three years. This devastation would have given Minoan colonies on the Greek mainland the opportunity to rise as masters and subordinate the culture that founded them.

The Mycenaeans did in fact absorb the earlier Minoan culture, and this scenario would explain the similarity in writing style and the apparent Anatolian roots of Mycenaean architecture, as well as meshing with the timing of the rise of Mycenaean civilization. Precise dating of the Santorini eruption has never been achieved, but the main Minoan city of Knossos was rebuilt around 1550 BC, giving an approximate time frame. Supporting this dating are writings from the reign of the Egyptian Pharaoh Ahmose I (circa 1560 – 1535 BC). Ahmose I is noted for significant rebuilding, requiring reopening of dormant materials sources, suggesting necessary repair of major damage to the Egyptian infrastructure. This is the most likely explanation we have for the origins of the Mycenaean Empire.

Archaeology has established the Mycenaeans as prolific traders. Mycenaean goods have been found from Mesopotamia to the British Isles. Notable among Mycenaean trade goods was a broad array of decorated pottery. The wide geographic spread of Mycenaean pottery and the yeoman efforts of archaeologists to catalog the progression of styles over centuries provide modern scholars with two critical tools. The first is a reliable means of dating by seriation where none would otherwise exist. The second is a method of tracing the movement of elements of Mycenaean civilization.

The Mycenaean Empire appears to have stretched, at least in outpost form, from Asia Minor to Italy. Testimony to a warrior culture comes from burial sites where the elite were often entombed with armor and highly decorated weapons. Evidence of participation in large scale military operations comes from decorative art and from written accounts such as one from Pylos that cited the amount of bronze received in terms of being sufficient for 5,000 arrow heads or 240 swords. This equates to more than half a ton of bronze allocated to one of many cities from one shipment. The Empire as whole would have invested massive amounts of bronze into military activities.

Contemporary written accounts of Mycenaean military action have not been found. Our primary insight comes from later writers whose work focused on the Trojan War. The work that survives is thought to date to the 7th and 8th Centuries BC, about 500 years after the fall of the Mycenaean Empire. The writings contain substantial elements of fiction, but are thought to derive from earlier tradition that preserves the general tenor of Mycenaean society.

Homer's *Iliad* portrays what today we would call a feudal society, presided over by a predominant lord to whom subordinate lords swore fealty. Agamemnon, the lord of the *Iliad*, rules by divine right (the counsel of Zeus). He ranges in personality from benefactor to petty tyrant, but always functions within a conservative set of unwritten rules governing the conduct of the society over which he presides. Lesser lords such as Achilles and Odysseus either disrupt or provide cohesion for the society. When the commoner Thersites dares to criticize Agamemnon in council, he is verbally abused and assaulted by Odysseus. This suggests a nervous elite ready to lash out at any threat to a precarious social order. The boasting of Nestor about his participation in battles against savage mountain tribes suggests that internal security was also an issue.

In addition to the well-known *Iliad* and *Odyssey*, we also have fragments and summary of the *Epic Cycle*, which covers the Trojan War more broadly. These support a picture of the Mycenaean Empire as a confederation of city-states, with one pre-eminent. It is not clear if a single city-state was pre-eminent throughout the life span of the empire. Contemporary Egyptian and Hittite sources contain occasional references to names that appear to be individual Mycenaean cities, also tending to buttress the view of a confederation.

We do have some insight into organization at the individual city level from contemporary Mycenaean writings unearthed at Pylos and Knossos. The city was ruled by a king, whose functions appear to have been military, administrative and religious. According to epic accounts of the Trojan War, Pylos was the city of King Nestor, an ally of King

Menelaus of Sparta. The city's ruined megaron is commonly referred to by modern scholars as the Palace of Nestor.

The primary assistant to the king appears to have been the commander of the city's army. Other members of the court were either land holders or warriors. Each city-state was subdivided into districts with a governor and vice-governor who oversaw communal life and enforced royal edict. Citizens were either freemen, apparently meaning members of the royal entourage, or people, meaning workers at the communal level. Slaves were either the property of the palace or assigned to specific deities. No distinct priest class has been identified.

The economy follows the general stratification above, with the primary options being either work done in the orbit of the palace, or entrepreneurial efforts. An individual could do both at the same time. General supervision was maintained by scribes, who distributed rations, recorded output and assigned work. Their records, intended at the time to be temporary, give a clear picture of work done at the palace level, and speak to a tightly structured hierarchy in the two cities of Pylos and Knossos for which we have contemporary written information. Extrapolating to the remainder of the empire is an exercise in educated speculation, but for now it is all we have.

Archaeology has given us a physical picture of Mycenaean cities. Many were well fortified, often occupying dominant ground or, as at Mycenae, set against defensive terrain. As a trade-based society the Mycenaeans also required more accessible and therefore less defense-oriented establishments on the coastal plains.

Central to the city was the palace, which served as an administrative center and storage area for the wealth of the king as well as the royal residence. Palaces were laid out as rooms around a series of courtyards and in some cases, particularly Pylos, appear to have been built in more than one story. Close to the palace were the larger residences of the city, some reaching more than one hundred feet on a side and similarly set out as rooms around central courtyards, which likely served as living quarters and administrative centers for the city's aristocracy. Lesser citizens were relegated to rectangular structures of about half these dimensions, which were simply divided into rooms and lacked the courtyards and other amenities of the palace and related buildings. This supports the written portrait of a stratified society with a tightly clustered elite.

Archaeological finds speak to a high level of artisanship in the manufacture of decorative goods, and to significant civil engineering knowledge reflected in the construction of cities. The walls were known by later Greeks as cyclopean, based on the belief that only the mythical giant Cyclops had the strength to move the massive, unworked boulders used to construct them. The largest single stone piece yet found is the lintel of a grave site near Mycenae, estimated to weigh over one hundred tons and rivaling anything found in contemporary Egypt.

The Mycenaeans, like the Egyptians, made use of the corbelled arch, a sophisticated piece of engineering capable of spreading the weight of monumental structures around openings, permitting passageways to the interior. Mycenaean nobles were buried in elaborate graves with exquisitely wrought treasures whose craftsmanship was on a par with that of the Egyptians and the Hittites. As with the Egyptians and the Hittites, all this was accomplishment, and not salvation. Before we can understand the collapse of the three empires, however, we need to understand how empires rise and flourish.

TABLE OF CORE SYLLABLES -- MYCENAEAN LINEAR B

	a		e		i		o		u	
	a	🝁	e	🝂	i	🝃	o	🝄	u	🝅
d	da	🝆	de	🝇	di	🝈	do	🝉	du	🝊
j	ja	🝋	je	🝌			jo	🝍		
k	ka	⊕	ke	🝎	ki	🝏	ko	🝐	ku	🝑
m	ma	🝒	me	🝓	mi	🝔	mo	🝕	mu	🝖
n	na	🝗	ne	🝘	ni	🝙	no	🝚	nu	🝛
p	pa	🝜	pe	🝝	pi	🝞	po	🝟	pu	🝠
q	qa	🝡	qe	⊜	qi	🝢	qo	🝣		
r	ra	🝤	re	🝥	ri	🝦	ro	🝧	ru	🝨
s	sa	🝩	se	🝪	si	🝫	so	🝬	su	🝭
t	ta	🝮	te	🝯	ti	🝰	to	🝱	tu	🝲
w	wa	🝳	we	🝴	wi	🝵	wo	🝶		
z	za	🝷	ze	🝸			zo	🝹		

Empire Building 101

THE SIMULTANEOUS COLLAPSE OF THE three great Eastern Mediterranean Empires of the Late Bronze Age was rooted in the fundamental nature of empires, how they are built and how they are maintained. Catastrophic events played no role. Famine, earthquake and virus are common throughout history. Society has always recovered. The collapse of empires is specifically related to the structure of empires.

The *New Oxford American Dictionary* defines empire as *an extensive group of states or countries under a single supreme authority*. Extensive should be seen as relative to the transport capabilities of the time. The empires we are examining appear minuscule in an age when we can hurl nuclear thunderbolts between continents. In their day they were vast beyond the comprehension of most of their inhabitants. The obstacles to their formation and survival were daunting.

The definition provides the two main concepts of empire. First, empires are built up out of existing political units. Political units tend to coalesce around common culture, religion and language. These groupings tend to be cohesive and exclusive. Empires made up of such units are subject to fracture along pre-existing political or cultural fault lines. Second, and following logically, the creation and continuation of an empire depends on the skill of a ruling elite in providing the military, diplomatic and economic incentives to keep the units aligned under a single authority. Since both empires and their component states involve rule by a small elite, we need to understand how the few come to dominate the many.

From time immemorial the survival and ascension of man has depended on projectile delivery. Early man found himself at a competitive disadvantage in a world of much stronger animals. Even a chimpanzee, for example, can exert approximately seven times the strength of an adult male human. Accurately placed stones or thrown spears allowed engagement at stand-off range, where a territorial animal's natural strength or a predator's claws could not be brought to bear.

The physics of projectile delivery provided an additional advantage to the facile mind of man. Impact increases only in direct proportion to an increase in the mass of the projectile but it increases as the square of an increase in velocity. This allowed comparatively weak man to multiply his advantage through the use of spears thrown with the aid of mechanical leverage, stones propelled by centripetal accelerating slings and arrows launched with tension bows.

The same principles also tend to equalize strength differentials among humans, both physical and numerical. Weaker men with superior skill and guile might overcome stronger. Smaller groups might, with superior weapons and well-conceived and executed tactics, successfully challenge larger.

The oldest currently known evidence of the use of sophisticated projectile weapons in organized conflict predates 7,000 BC. A mass burial site has been unearthed in Egypt in which the remains contain what appear to be embedded arrow points. Cave paintings have been found in Algeria which show groups of men who appear to be archers in conflict. Neither interpretation is entirely free from controversy, but indications are strong that a mechanism by which few could dominate many was in already in place as civilization began its growth and spread.

The first steps toward empire were taken before recorded history but we can make educated guesses based on behavior common across cultures during the historic period. Competition for scarce resources in the form of arable land and domesticated animals would have led to violent confrontations. The power of village and tribal leaders would depend on their ability to prevail.

Leaders with designs on neighboring resources would have faced restrictions. Manpower needed for aggression was also needed to tend flocks and crops. War could be conducted only on a seasonal basis, between harvest and planting. This pattern persisted into the Imperial Era of the Late Bronze Age. The Egyptians, whose activities we can date precisely, began major campaigns shortly after the conclusion of harvest.

Even in season, only a portion of the available manpower could be sent out to battle. Sending everyone would leave the aggressor's own animals and food stocks exposed to brigands and beasts of prey. It was a delicate balancing act. Send out too few and you would risk defeat. Send too many and you might return to find your own resources plundered, your populace carried off into slavery and your domicile reduced to smoldering rubble.

In order to make appropriate resource allocations, leaders needed sufficient information to assess the strengths and weaknesses of potential adversaries, not only to mount aggressive action but also to determine what defense works might be needed to protect their own physical infrastructure. In modern terms, they needed reconnaissance and espionage.

Reconnaissance may have been as simple as neighborly visits and the hosting of feasts to size up those in their vicinity. The second would have been more insidious; gathering gossip from traders and merchants, dispatching agents in various guises, leveraging family connections where available. By the Late Bronze Age espionage had been refined to a high art, but even in the days before metal and wheeled vehicles, warfare would have been a complex undertaking.

Once the composition of forces had been worked out, issues of logistics had to be addressed. Supplies of food and water had to be sufficient for the march to and from the selected target. A store of projectiles sufficient to overcome the defenders would be needed. If the combined load was too heavy or bulky for individual fighters to carry, dedicated transport would be required. Some sort of medical corps would be needed to tend to the wounded.

Beyond complexity lay two forms of risk. First, manpower losses in an unsuccessful raid could cripple the economy of the raiders and degrade their capability to defend themselves. Second, even a successful foray could cost more to prosecute than it returned in booty, leaving the aggressors worse off in spite of victory.

Any society ambitious enough to progress beyond seizing resources to conquest faced an exponentially larger set of challenges. Raiders needed only to displace the defenders from land or hold them at bay long enough to make off with any available booty. Conquest involved investiture and long term subjugation. This required a force of dedicated infantry serving on a year round basis, as well as supporting projectile delivery capability in the event of organized rebellion.

The accumulation of manpower required for conquest was accomplished either by a draft system that levied a certain time of military obligation on all citizens, after which they would return to the labor force, or by the creation of a military class within the citizenry to serve as a career army with no residual responsibilities.

Either approach entailed administrative overhead involving detailed personnel rosters, tables of organization and equipment, accrual and disbursement of pay and the other sundry record keeping necessary to maintain a military organization, as well as a chain of command to enable structure and discipline. This signals both an availability of manpower in excess of the subsistence needs of the population and the emergence of a stratified social system capable of organizing and supporting a division of labor under which military draft or specialization were viable.

Additional administrative overhead would be involved in the occupation of a conquered area. Some element of the conqueror's leadership would have to be dispatched to provide permanent governance and command the occupying military. Detailed economic records would be required to ensure the appropriate collection of taxes and tribute. Take too little and conquest is not worthwhile. Take too much and rebellion becomes inevitable. Since the conquered entity's social infrastructure would not vanish overnight, an element of diplomacy would be needed to gain whatever cooperation might be available.

With governance came additional risk. Those appointed to watch over the conquered populace would always be tempted to seize control and secede. Subordinate administrators might well have ambitions to oust the current leadership. Ties of blood and marriage provided no security. The Hittites were plagued by familial homicide. The Egyptian Pharaoh Ramses III was assassinated in a plot hatched within his harem. One hero of the *Iliad,* Agamemnon, was murdered by his wife and her lover, while another, Odysseus, died at the hands of an illegitimate son. Internal security apparatus would be essential to mitigate these perils.

Expansion beyond the territory of an immediate neighbor compounded the aggressor's difficulty out of proportion to growth. Not only were the problems replicated with each conquest, but adding new territory to the domain of existing bureaucracies meant that any inefficiency or corruption was magnified across the entire realm. Each success made the next more difficult. The conqueror would be compelled to deploy an increasing percentage of his forces to defend territory already seized, thus reducing the available assault force. It would become obvious to those in the would-be conqueror's path that they would soon be on his agenda, leading to the formation of defensive alliances. The conqueror would require an ever more efficient military establishment. Increased reliance on organization, training and projectile delivery would be needed to offset any numerical disadvantage.

Expansion to the size of a nation-state presented the additional problem of distance. With the exception of the Egyptians, who had the Nile at hand to facilitate movement of forces, would-be conquerors were reduced to long marches over caravan tracks to reach their objectives. Extensive labor would be needed to move the supplies required for a long campaign. Those supplies would have to be under constant guard to prevent their loss to opportunistic marauders. Effective organization would be essential. Administrative overhead would be magnified.

The leap from kingdom to empire introduced barriers of complexity and distance that required technological advances to enhance transport, assault superiority and administration. The earliest evidence for the two key components, wheeled conveyance and written language, places their origins somewhere in the 4th Millennium BC. While we are on somewhat shaky logical ground basing origins on the simple lack of currently available evidence of something earlier, we do at least know these components were in place in the early stages of the Bronze Age late in the 4th Millennium BC.

An understanding of the nature of Bronze and its place in Eastern Mediterranean civilization will give us perhaps the best insight into the empires that depended on it. The metal as used at that time was a straightforward alloy of copper and tin. The two component metals presented different but daunting problems.

Copper was smelted from an ore called malachite, which tends to occur in vertical seams. Copper forms only about 10% of the ore. In order to refine usable amounts of copper, great amounts of ore had to be lifted considerable vertical distances out of narrow mine shafts. The melting point of the metal is 1,984 degrees Fahrenheit. To reach this temperature requires charcoal and some sort of blast furnace effect, probably created by bellows.

The calorie value of wood varies by type, but it is not unreasonable to suggest that 250 pounds of wood were consumed to smelt each pound of copper from native ore. Progressive deforestation around the workings would require that wood be retrieved from greater and greater distances. Once the smelt was complete, vast amounts of slag had to be hauled away and dumped where it would not get in the way of smelting operations. This required a sizeable labor force, which had to be organized, supervised, fed, clothed and housed.

Tin presented another problem. The ore of tin available to Late Bronze Age miners was cassiterite (stannous dioxide, chemically SnO_2). Deposits are known in Eastern Egypt, but were not worked. Other potential tin sources are Bohemia to the north, Cornwall in England and Afghanistan. The Bohemian deposits occurred as seams in hard granite, and would have been difficult to recover with the technology of the time. Distance from the Eastern Mediterranean made Cornwall problematic. By default, the most likely source of tin used in the Eastern Mediterranean was Afghanistan. Whatever the source, obtaining tin required a sophisticated international trade and economic structure capable of providing the metal in industrial quantities. Trade routes would be critical.

Weapons grade bronze required about 10% tin to achieve proper toughness. Bronze used for armor was usually around 6% tin, allowing it to be more easily beaten into plates. Proportions for other uses varied widely, probably more dependent on the availability of tin than anything else. This required both metallurgical facilities capable of producing the correct metals and craftsmen skilled enough to work them into finished products.

At the opening of the 3rd Millennium BC we see the kind of technological sophistication, social organization and international economic cooperation that would, some centuries, later underpin the earliest empire.

SARGON OF AKKAD

THE EARLIEST RECOGNIZABLE EMPIRE EMERGED in ancient Mesopotamia, essentially modern Iraq. Human habitation in the area dates back to co-existence with Neanderthals. The Neolithic Revolution, about 9000 BC, brought a change in life style. Three primary elements emerged, urbanization, agriculture and the domestication of animals. Historians are fond of thinking in terms of cause and effect. Variously it has been proposed that domestication came first and required agriculture to feed the animals, that agriculture came first and freed populations in excess of those required to tend crops to cluster in cities and pursue crafts, and most recently that cities came first, growing up around religious sites and requiring agriculture to support them and the domestication of animals for ritual sacrifice.

None of the three theories can be proven or disproven. We simply lack evidence. We don't know when agriculture and domestication began because it requires time for plants and animals to evolve as a result of cultivation and domestication. Archaeologists exploring this period cannot tell the residue of wild crops from cultivated or the bones of wild animals from domestic, even when finds can be reliably dated. While this also prevents the order of emergence of cities from being determined, we are able to deduce a great deal from urban ruins.

Cities are basic to the growth of empire. They are the core of the states that will be brought under a single ruler. The earliest recognizable city we know of is located at Catal Huyuk, covering some 32 acres in the southern part of modern Turkey. It is made up of individual mud brick houses with no streets or courtyards, and no space to pass between them. Entrance was through the roof, reached by ladder. The first line of defense against predators or invaders was to deny entrance by raising the ladders. Caves were a common cooperative dwelling of refuge during the earlier phases Stone Age. Catal Huyuk has something of the look of a vast do-it-yourself cave. The presence of mineral resources in the area may suggest that mining was a component of the economy. We know nothing of the culture or mode of governance at Catal Huyuk.

We know of Jericho from Judeo-Christian scripture. The city is notable for three things. First is its famous wall, which in the Neolithic era rose about twelve feet. Whether it was built as a defense against marauders or to protect mud brick dwellings from rising flood waters is not known. Construction of the wall required organization, supervision and communal labor, all essential to later empire building. Second, the city is not organized as a unit, but appears to be built in clusters of dwellings, perhaps segregated by kinship. This suggests an ability to form cooperative alliances. Third, archaeologists have found obsidian, a volcanic glass highly prized for its ability to take and hold a sharp edge, which has been traced to a source hundreds of miles north in modern Turkey. This is concrete evidence of long range trade, which requires knowledge of distant cultures and the existence of routes that can be followed by would-be empire builders.

The earliest Mesopotamian city we know about is Uruk, located south of modern Baghdad on what was then a channel of the Euphrates River. Excavations have identified layers of settlements on the site, one built on top of another. The oldest has been dated by sedimentary stratification to about 5000 BC. From about 4000 BC and through the following 4th Millennium Uruk grew into a major urban center in the modern sense, with specialization of labor, stratification of society and dedicated bureaucratic, religious and military establishments. Increased sophistication contributed to the need for a refined system of writing and record keeping, thought to have fully developed by around 3200 BC. Through sponsorship, alliance or domination, the city exercised considerable influence over surrounding cities and villages, qualifying as what modern scholars refer to as a city-state. Uruk reached the height of its power and development around 2900 BC.

Climate studies have established that annual rainfall totals in Mesopotamia declined during the 3rd Millennium BC to approximately modern levels. Agriculture came to depend on the annual floods of the

Tigris and Euphrates rivers, which could vary considerably depending on accumulated volumes and natural timing of release in the rivers' watersheds. Some historians suggest that diminished rainfall and the corresponding reduction in arable land led to increased militarization in the 3rd Millennium BC to support competition for scarce resources. While the cause may be the subject of speculation, the fact of military activity is established by both contemporary writing and archaeological evidence.

During the 3rd Millennium BC city-states expanded. Their rulers fought regularly to establish boundaries and defend against incursion. Legend has Gilgamesh, the God-King of Uruk, building a defensive wall around the city. The *Epic of Gilgamesh* is thought to date from around 2700 BC. Uruk's wall can still be traced today, and measures more than five miles in length. The bricks of the wall were individually kiln-fired, a massive undertaking requiring organization and a significant commitment of resources.

No wall or military activity would resolve the shortfall in fertility. The impact of diminished rainfall could only be mitigated by construction of man-made systems of irrigation to make the most effective use of available river flow. Massive irrigation involved a latticework of canals, ditches and feeder channels, all of which had to be laboriously built and scrupulously maintained. This labor intensive feat of civil engineering is further evidence of a high order of social organization.

Written records from Mesopotamia's 3rd Millennium BC come to us in two languages, Sumerian and Akkadian. These were the languages of the two main groups competing for resources in Mesopotamia at the time. The Sumerian culture and economy were based on agriculture. The Akkadians, Semitic herdsmen thought to have migrated from the North, coveted the land under Sumerian cultivation to graze their animals. Both languages were rendered in a script called cuneiform, after the general wedge shape of the characters. Records and other documents were commonly baked into clay tablets over the many centuries the languages were in use.

Cuneiform tablets survive today in their tens of thousands, providing a detailed look at life thousands of years ago. Writing ranges from school books to pharmacists' formularies, from mundane business transactions to royal letters.

The transliteration of cuneiform tablets is no trivial undertaking. The writing is largely pictographic, with a wide variety of symbols. The first step is to resolve the often deteriorated scratching on the clay. This may require advanced and very expensive scanning techniques. The second is to break the complex code of the symbols. The third is to render the encoded ancient language into a modern language. A single tablet can take weeks or months of effort. Many of the tablets and clay cylinders from the period are still waiting to be read.

While details continue to emerge, we do have a broad general picture of the period. By the middle of the 3rd Millennium BC, Mesopotamia had evolved into a patchwork of city-states. Expansion could come only at the expense of adjoining realms. The map shifted in response to the prevailing balance of power. It wasn't until the latter portion of the 3rd Millennium BC that a single ruler was able to conquer and consolidate the small realms.

Among the surviving documents is the autobiography of Sargon, the founder of the Akkadian Empire. In it he claims no knowledge of his father and little more of his mother, who sealed her infant son in a basket and set him adrift on the river Euphrates. This could have been a means of divesting himself of inconvenient parentage or, since the framers of Judeo-Christian scripture used essentially the same narrative for Moses in *Exodus*, it may have been homage to an earlier and now lost tradition. Either way, we see a man careful of his legend in the later years of his life.

In his earlier years Sargon was a member of the court of the king of the city of Kish, with specific responsibility for maintaining the city's complex of irrigation channels. Kish was located about fifty miles south of modern Baghdad on a tributary of the Euphrates River. Control of irrigation at this point gave the city significant economic impact on surrounding areas and gave the city's ruler influence in places where he did not have outright dominion. Sargon was able to displace his patron and become king himself, laying the foundation for the Akkadian Empire.

We do not know where Akkad was located. Contemporary writing establishes that it was a city, but the time and treasure invested by archaeologists in searching for its remains have produced nothing. We are also in the dark as to Sargon's military training and background. While we don't know specifically what military capability he commanded, we do have some insight into the state of Mesopotamian military organization around the time of his ascension.

The most often cited source for military organization in mid 3rd Millennium BC Mesopotamia is the *Stela of Vultures*, erected by a king of the city of Lagash to celebrate his victory over a neighboring kingdom. Pictorial representations on the Stela show clear indications of armored and well-equipped men drawn up in what appear to be fighting ranks. This is generally taken to indicate the presence of a professional military, since fighting in formation requires training and discipline beyond that available from an army of citizen soldiers campaigning only between harvesting and planting seasons. Uniformity of equipment suggests centralized logistics and standardized tactics, further indications of a professional military establishment.

The preponderance of foot soldiers on the *Stela of Vultures* suggests that forces configured to seize and hold territory were common by Sargon's time. An inscription from the Stela refers to a rival king being struck by an arrow. This, supported by other written and visual portrayals from the period, suggests a style of war in which projectile weapons such as bows, slings and javelins were followed up by massed infantry assault with spears and axes. Chariots of the time were clumsy, four-wheeled affairs that appear to have served mainly as conveyances for the elite.

Sargon is said to have had 5,400 men permanently at his disposal. These are widely assumed to be a military cadre, but what specific roles they fulfilled are not recorded. He would have required a much larger force to prosecute even his earliest campaign against the city of Uruk.

Uruk lay some distance to the south of Kish and was pre-eminent among a group of surrounding cities. In launching his campaign against Uruk, Sargon was moving toward seizing control of an existing power bloc, rather than engaging in the land grabs and flare-ups of inter-city strife that preceded his efforts. With Uruk and its vassal cities under his control, Sargon spent the next few years bringing the remaining cities of Mesopotamia into his dominion.

Sargon's vision was not limited to the Tigris and Euphrates valleys. Following consolidation of Mesopotamia, he expanded to the east, north and west. In contemporary writing, Sargon often referred to his conquests in terms of the primary resources which came under his control as a result; tin from Elam, the southwestern portion of what is now Iran, silver from the Taurus Mountains to the north in modern Turkey and cedars from the Mediterranean region to the west.

In order to understand the success of the Akkadian Empire, and other empires, we must look beyond the initial military engagements that resulted in the conquest of the member states. Conquest by itself could not guarantee imperial integrity. The key to welding disparate, hostile elements together was the development of a robust, integrated economy that provided the resources for production and expedited trade in the goods produced. If conquered populations were starving under the yoke of empire, they would have nothing to lose by rebellion. If empire brought prosperity, conquest would be palatable to the majority. They had always been subject to despotic rule anyway. The few remaining malcontents could be dealt with by the same apparatus that secured the empire against external threat. A robust economy was necessary to pay for a robust security apparatus.

The sheer size of Sargon's conquests raised the need for physical and administrative infrastructure to new levels. He built an internal road network to support commerce and military deployment, commissioned a postal service to augment and control communication and installed the Akkadian language as the standard for diplomacy and commerce. The Sumerian language seems to have remained as the upper class and religious mode of communication, perhaps as a permissible form of rebellion to placate the displaced elite.

The imposition of Akkadian as a uniform language across Mesopotamia and the Eastern Mediterranean was Sargon's most persistent legacy. It was a thousand years after the fall of the Akkadian empire before Akkadian cuneiform began to be replaced as the written mode of communication in Eastern Mediterranean trade and inter-state diplomacy. This has been a boon to modern researchers, who are able to read inter-cultural exchanges even in cases where native languages are lost or native written material has not survived.

The Akkadian Empire itself is a testament to Sargon's personal skill as a military commander, diplomat and administrator. No one before him had been able to amass the number of serial battlefield victories necessary to assemble enough component states to make an empire, nor develop the level of economic and political stability necessary to hold a vastly superior number of ambitious rulers under his sway. His vision of the empire as a whole was rare, if not unique, and the physical and administrative infrastructure he built to realize that vision had no peer up to his time.

The weakness of Sargon's empire lay in his personal strength. Following his death no successor could muster the combination of intellect, vision and force of personality required to hold together what he had amassed. The disintegration of the Akkadian empire occurred within a century of Sargon's death. Cuneiform tablets of the time complain of food shortages and hyper-inflation. Tribal uprisings among conquered cultures and barbarian pressure from the East brought military reverses. Whether these were the cause or the result of resource shortages, or whether the two were intertwined in some fatal ballet, is not clear. We have snippets of detail from the economy of the time, but we do not have a clear picture of the overall economic structure of the Akkadian Empire. We can only infer its importance from the consequences of its failure.

In spite of its collapse, the Akkadian Empire set a new standard of ambition in the regions where it had held sway and offered a blueprint for those who wanted to follow in Sargon's footsteps. Urban centers did come to rule considerable fiefdoms. One king of the city of Ur declared himself *Ruler of Sumer and Akkad*, but no single authority was able to duplicate the extent of Sargon's conquests. It would be another 700 years before the Egyptian, Hittite and Mycenaean Empires rose to exercise similar dominion, in lands distant from Mesopotamia.

IMPERIAL ARMS AND ARMIES

Eᴍᴘɪʀᴇ ʙᴇɢɪɴs ᴡɪᴛʜ ᴄᴏɴQᴜᴇsᴛ. A robust economy, skillful administration and adroit diplomacy may be essential in holding the disparate member states together once imperial authority has been established, but their initial subjugation requires force of arms.

During the centuries following the collapse of the Akkadian Empire military technology continued to evolve. Projectile delivery, a key component of imperial superiority, benefitted dramatically from the development of the two-wheel war chariot during the last half of the 2nd Millennium BC. Mechanical engineering and materials science progressed to the point where it was possible to produce a light-weight sprung vehicle that provided a stable and maneuverable archery platform from which to deploy the premier assault weapon of the day, the composite, recurve bow.

Imperial archives from the Late Bronze Age make it clear that the chariot was of paramount military importance, but we do not know exactly how it was used. No contemporary manual for the tactical employment of chariots has survived. We can, however, make some general suppositions based on known parameters. We will focus on the Egyptian model, which is the best known.

Both contemporary illustrations and surviving examples show the chariot was designed as a mobile archery platform. Modern tests performed on accurately constructed replicas confirm this. Contrary to film portrayals, the Egyptian war chariot of the Late Bronze Age was small and light enough for two men to lift and carry for a short distance. Rather than employing mass and structural rigidity, the vehicle was built with the flexibility needed to maintain stability at speed over uneven ground. The wheels are spoked rather than solid to reduce unsprung weight. Most wheels were of six spoke design, which is the minimum required to prevent deflection of the rim. Harnessing for the two horse tandem was minimal. Armor and decoration were omitted. Drawings do not show large numbers of arrows carried in a single vehicle. The ratio of about ten arrows per bow found in the tomb of Pharaoh Tutankhamen appears to be a possible norm.

High mobility and low war load per vehicle suggests a quick strike-and-retreat philosophy in chariot employment. This philosophy is also consistent with the fact that both horses and crews would dehydrate rapidly in hot Middle-Eastern battle conditions. In order to maintain pressure on opposing forces, the chariots might have moved in waves, with one attacking while others were taking on water and arrows. Under such a tactical regime, 1,500 chariots could deliver up to 15,000 arrows with reasonable accuracy in each complete pass, with multiple passes available as necessary.

Surviving after action reports provide an additional clue to the imperial use of chariots. Contemporary Egyptian records of capture of live enemy horses show a ratio of two horses per enemy chariot taken. The live capture ratio indicates that chariot horses were not routinely exposed to opposing projectiles or weapons. The popular concept of chariot deployment in which skirmish lines of chariots charge into massed opposing infantry to terrorize troops and break up formations is inaccurate. The horses drawing the oncoming chariots would have provided inviting targets for archers, javelin throwers and slingers. If chariots were used to break the main line of infantry resistance, the horses would have been further exposed to spears, swords and axes. They would have suffered disproportionately large casualties.

Hittite chariots differed somewhat from the Egyptian model in that they were built to carry a crew of three, rather than the two man crew of driver and archer common in Egypt. The third crew member is generally depicted as being armed with a spear. The spears in surviving pictorial representations appear to be configured for stabbing rather than throwing. None are long enough to project forward of the chariot horses for use like a medieval lance. The spear bearer probably served to defend the chariot in the event that it became entangled with opposing infantry in the confusion of battle.

Actual construction of the chariot may have differed also. Some contemporary Egyptian drawings suggest the Hittite version placed the axle a little aft of the center of the vehicle. Other Egyptian drawings represent the Hittite chariot with the axle in the full aft position. It is possible both designs were used. It is also possible that some Egyptian artists never saw an actual Hittite chariot and simply drew three occupants in the standard Egyptian model.

Less is known about Mycenaean chariots. Records from the city of Pylos establish that a chariot corps existed at the city level and address the ownership of both vehicles and horses. Homer's *Iliad* contains numerous mentions of chariots. A Trojan prince is cited as carrying a spear of just less than nineteen feet in length. Such a spear would project forward of the chariot horses and could be used as a lance. Tactical chariot use during the Trojan War was limited and does not shed any light on their employment in formation. Archery was the province of men on foot whose primary armament was the bow.

Bows are categorized according to both style and method of construction. The earliest and simplest bows are the straight or self type, of which the English long bow is an example. The launch velocity of a bow increases with its draw length (maximum extension of the bow). In a self bow, draw length increases in proportion to the length of the bow. At some point overall length makes this design unwieldy. The later recurve or compound curve bow is bent backward at the ends, allowing greater draw length in a shorter bow.

In both types the bowstring is drawn back manually, producing compressive stress on the rear or inside of the bow and tensile stress on the front (target-facing) side of the bow. When the bowstring is released, the tension is converted into launch force against the rear or nock portion of the arrow and (in accordance with Newton's law) an equal and opposite recoil against the archer's hand.

The first issue facing the bow maker was locating or constructing a material that would properly store and release opposing stresses. In the self bow this was solved by selection of bow material, usually a piece of wood comprised of stiff (inert) heartwood that would handle compressive stresses, surrounded by elastic (active) sapwood to deal with tensile stresses. Care had to be taken during manufacture to preserve the existing grain. Any separation could cause failure.

The earliest efforts at improvement involved gluing animal sinew, which has about four times the tensile strength of wood, to the arms of bows to handle tensile stresses. The next step was to glue horn, often that of water buffalo, to the inside or belly of the bow, which offered about twice the power of heart wood to deal with compressive stresses. Horn had the ability to return to its original shape following deformation during the draw of the bow. This was the basis of the composite bow.

The increased power of the bow increased recoil. The natural psychological reaction of the archer would be to anticipate the recoil and tighten various muscle groups, disturbing his aim. This is the same as a shooter flinching before the discharge of a modern firearm. Basic physics offered two solutions. The first was to increase the weight of the bow. Felt recoil is inversely proportional to the square of the weight of the bow. The second was to fashion a large handgrip in the middle of the bow to spread the force of recoil over a greater area and diminish the shock. Neither solution was elegant; both were limited by practical considerations.

The version used by the Egyptian forces in the Late Bronze Age was an ingenious style called Asiatic Angular, and appears as a flat triangle at rest. The angle (central hold point) of the bow did not deflect when the bow was drawn, so that all the force of release was absorbed by movement of the arms of the bow and there was no recoil into the archer's hand, promoting accurate shooting.

The performance of Egyptian bows is cited in units of measure common to the time. A cubit was the distance from the elbow to the fingertips. Standard bars recovered from Egypt and Mesopotamia average about twenty and a half inches. The next measure down was the palm, as in palm of the hand. The smallest on this scale was the finger. Bow range was a maximum of 550 cubits, just more than 300 yards in modern parlance. Maximum penetration was said to be a thickness of three fingers of copper.

Later statistics tend to support Egyptian claims for range and penetration. The record for range from a composite recurve bow using a flight (lightweight) arrow is approximately one half mile. Standards for medieval English long bow archers called for them to be able to hit a bale of hay at 440 yards. Their war (heavier) arrows were able to penetrate the armor of French knights at the battle of Agincourt. Assuming comparable results from Late Bronze Age weapons, the Egyptian army went into the field with daunting projectile delivery capability.

This sort of mechanical marvel required a high level of skill to produce. Setting of the laminates could require long periods. The time elapsed between the arrival of raw materials at the bow maker and completion of the weapon could be five years. Arrows with proper aerodynamics and accuracy required precise turning, fletching, nocking and pointing. Volume manufacture called for a significant infrastructure.

Probably for reasons of either economy or availability, wooden self bows remained in use, rather than being entirely superseded by the composite bow. The inventory of grave goods from the burial of Pharaoh Tutankhamen included 32 angular composite bows, 14 self bows and 430 arrows. We do not know the tactical mix in field use, but various pictorial representations suggest that self bows were common among foot archers while composite bows appear more frequently in depictions of chariot archers.

Chariot archery added a significant level of complexity to military organization. Archers, drivers and horses all had to be specially trained. According to contemporary Hittite records, the training of a team of chariot horses alone required about seven months. Individual proficiency and skill in tactical maneuver required constant exercise to maintain. Chariot capabilities had to be integrated tactically with the infantry capability necessary to seize and hold ground. Examining the Egyptian model, we find a two tiered structure. The chariot forces comprised an elite, usually enrolled by name in recognition of individual importance. Infantry forces were recorded by number, suggesting that foot soldiers were drawn from lower social classes.

The foot soldier of the time was small by modern standards, ranging in height from 5 feet 3 inches to 5 feet 6 inches and in weight from 125 to 150 pounds. Primary armaments for regular Egyptian soldiers were the spear, bronze tipped lance and about a foot longer than the wielder was tall, and the sickle sword, named for its curved blade, although the cutting edge was on the outside rather than on the inside as with the farm implement.

Infantry training included no-holds-barred wrestling (something akin to modern unlimited fighting), weight-lifting and distance running. Individual combat training appears to have been done as a form of stick fighting, rather than with the use of actual edged or pointed weapons. Training in tactical maneuver and formation fighting would also have been required.

The infantry core of the Egyptian Army was organized in numerical blocks to facilitate supervision and tactical deployment. The lowest level was a squad, consisting of ten men. Five squads made a platoon of 50 men and five platoons made a company of 250 men. Two companies made a host of 500 men. The largest maneuver element was the division, consisting of 5,000 men and often named for one of Egypt's many gods.

Depending upon immediate military needs, the Egyptian Army also included contingents of foreign fighters. Some were sourced from battlefield capture. Soldiers on the losing side were given the option to bring their military skills to the Egyptian Army. Other foreign fighters were hired as mercenaries. Nubians were widely used as foot archers and scouts. The later Greek historian Herodotus writes of men of bronze selling their fighting skills to the Pharaohs of Egypt, suggesting that city-states of the Mycenaean Empire derived part of their income from providing troops to the Egyptian Army.

Command of the larger elements of the Egyptian Army was not placed in the hands of a professional military. Based on contemporary accounts of careers, senior officials moved relatively freely between civilian and military leadership positions. Military skills may have been developed and honed across the entire elite by service in a series of increasingly responsible junior positions. The Pharaoh, who was in overall command of the army in both garrison and campaign situations, was expected to display skill in generalship in addition to his many other administrative and ceremonial duties.

The Hittite Empire also employed a pyramidal military organization and command structure. Command seems to have progressed in decimal increments (10, 100, etc.) and fallen to members of the elite. Mercenaries were used as needed. The Hittites relied more heavily than the Egyptians on forces drawn from vassal states. Unlike the Egyptian and Hittite models, Mycenaean military structure existed at the city level. When a larger force was needed, it was assembled as a feudal confederation.

Weapons differed in style among the Empires, and evolved over time in response to technological advances and situational necessity. Two categories prevailed. Projectile delivery involved bows, javelins and slings. Close combat required spears, swords, axes and clubs.

These were the arms and armies that forged the Late Bronze Age empires of the Eastern Mediterranean.

IMPERIAL CAMPAIGNS

T HE LATE BRONZE AGE USE of chariot archery in sufficient mass to achieve large scale victory was a challenging feat of tactics, administration and logistics. In order to serve as a tool of empire building, it had to be performed repeatedly under the most difficult conditions imaginable. The first detailed account of an imperial campaign that we have comes to us from the Pharaoh Thutmoses III, who commissioned a narrative of his victory at Megiddo in the Mid 15th Century BC. This narrative survives on the walls of the Temple of Amun at the city of Karnak. Completed in the later years of Thutmoses III's reign, but still within living memory of events, it qualifies as contemporary writing.

Thutmoses III succeeded to the throne following the death of his stepmother and co-regent, Hatshepsut. Her focus as regent had been commerce with areas to the south of Egypt rather than maintenance of the empire in Canaan. Thutmoses III's first challenge was a revolt led by the King of the city of Megiddo. Megiddo was located in what is now central Israel and controlled the main trade route between Egypt and Mesopotamia. It was long a strategic prize and was the site of battles as recently as World War I. Today a paved thoroughfare runs in the shadow of the ruins of the city. In Thutmoses III's time, Megiddo was the center of a general revolt by tribes in the area of Canaan. The revolt was supported by the King of Kadesh, a key Syrian city, and may have had tacit if not outright material support from the Kingdom of Mitanni. It was, in short, a major threat to Egyptian interests in Canaan.

Thutmoses III's campaign narrative is something along the lines of a modern military after-action report. It focuses on the tactical aspects of the campaign and tends to be terse in regard to pedestrian details. The narrative does, however, contain the oldest surviving mention of combat use of the composite bow.

The battle was fought, according to Egyptian records, on the 21st day of the first month of the third season of the 23rd year of Thutmoses III's reign. The year was probably 1456 BC, although this is of less importance to our understanding than the month. The date given equates to April. The grain harvest schedule in Middle Kingdom Egypt finished at the end of March. Some scholars suggest that this timing permitted the levy of military age males who would otherwise be needed for farming to fill out the Egyptian army. This seems unlikely. A professional chariot based army required a background of rigorous drill in weapons and tactics. There would be little use for raw recruits in a major campaign.

Conscription worked in the opposite direction. Members of the military appear to have been levied on occasion to assist in the annual harvest. This practice has persisted into modern times. The 1950 AD invasion of agrarian South Korea by the industrial North was timed for late June, when the greatest number of South Korean soldiers had been given leave to work in the rice paddies. Any civilian levy for Thutmoses III's Egyptian army was probably to fill out the logistics train and provide unskilled labor. Shortages in combat specialties would be addressed by hiring experienced mercenaries. The number of mercenaries required would have made it impractical to recruit on an individual basis. They would have been hired in groups, most likely with a command structure in place.

Since the mercenary forces were foreign sourced, there was potential for misunderstanding due to language differences. This would have been magnified under combat stress and might imperil the outcome of an engagement. This argues for a single source for mercenary forces, or at least multiple sources fluent in the same language, so that a minimum of translation would be required.

We have previously noted that the 5th Century BC Greek historian Herodotus speaks of men of bronze selling their skill in battle to the Pharaohs of Egypt. Herodotus was not a historian in the modern sense of a disciplined researcher, but often culled material from older stories passed down through an unknown number of generations; what we would call lore. This suggests a tradition that some of the Egyptian mercenaries were Mycenaean. Neither Herodotus nor contemporary Egyptian documentation address numbers, composition or method of payment.

Beyond the issue of language, there was the potential with any heavily armed force for rogue behavior. The best insurance against this would be to recruit through the kings of cities outside the Empire who would provide the requisite trained and armed young men, but who would hold dominion over the families of those they sent, creating control through a de-facto hostage situation. This would also simplify payment. Any wages due could be sent to the kings, who would then pay the mercenaries in local specie, goods or privileges. That would leave the Egyptians with responsibility only for feeding the mercenary forces at their disposal.

Perhaps the main advantage of waiting until the harvest was complete was the availability of food supplies to support the expedition. Any ruler undertaking a major campaign was gambling with the food reserves of his nation. An unsuccessful effort coupled with a large investment in grain and other forms of nutrition could disastrously weaken the nation prosecuting the campaign. The risk was particularly acute for Egypt. In ancient times the Nile valley was the breadbasket of the Mediterranean. Egypt's prosperity rested on a surplus of grain to trade for the other commodities required to sustain the economy.

The subsistence agrarian economy of Egypt had, by the time of the New Kingdom, evolved into a system of sharecropping, in which most land was owned by the palace or various temples and worked by farmers who paid a fixed tax and kept any excess for themselves. This placed the burden of low yields on the farmers. In the event of crop failure, widespread starvation could destroy the essential labor base of the economy. The government would have to step in and feed the population from grain storage set aside for lean years. It would be in Thutmoses III's best interest to understand the overall food situation in Egypt and tailor his expeditionary force to leave behind sufficient reserves to insure against potential famine.

The size of Thutmoses III's force has been estimated at between 10,000 and 20,000. Composition is not known, but a rough breakdown is possible. Records of battlefield capture show 924 Canaanite chariots. Thutmoses III would not have had fewer. If we set a minimum of 1,500 two-man chariots, we can extrapolate to 3,000 chariot crew. Since chariot crew were elite members of the force and would presumably not engage in manual labor, we can further estimate supporting hostlers, repairmen and others based on a 1:3 ratio at about 1,000.

Chariots could not fight unsupported by infantry. The two man chariot crew, a driver and an archer, had limited armor and defensive arms. Infantry was required to protect the chariots and to exploit tactical success. The massive volume of arrows launched by chariot formations could create casualties and shatter the integrity of enemy formations, but the unpleasant work of mopping up and seizing ground could only be done by foot soldiers. There does not appear to be a set numerical ratio of infantry to chariots. Freedom to tailor force configuration to specific campaigns or engagements would have been an advantage for field commanders. The best available information would place two divisions, or 10,000 infantry, at Megiddo. Additional personnel would be needed to provide skilled services, manual labor and security for expedition's considerable logistics train.

The record of campaign provides an interesting confirmation of the size of the Egyptian battle force. The final approach to Megiddo was a high-risk transit through a ten mile long defile called the Aruna Pass. Since the topography had to accommodate two man chariots with wide tracks and protruding axles, there must have been room for infantry to march three abreast. The record says that the rear elements of Thutmoses III's army were just entering the pass as the lead elements were coming out the far end. Assuming a reasonably close interval of march, we can assign 20 lineal feet in the line of march for each chariot for a total of 30,000 lineal feet and 6 feet for each three man rank of infantry. 10,000 infantry would require a total of 20,000 lineal feet. This does approximate the 50,000 lineal feet in ten miles.

This massive army began its march some eleven days earlier from the Egyptian border city of Sile. The city was the departure point for land expeditions to the north, and may have served as an arming and disarming point for forces departing from and returning to Egypt.

Heavily armed groups within Egypt proper would have posed a threat to internal security.

From Sile north to Gaza, the nearest friendly city large enough to serve as a rest and resupply point for a major expedition, required a march of 10 days. This took place on dirt tracks through arid country in relentless heat. Adding to this misery, the dust clouds stirred up by the lead men and animals in Thutmoses III's column would have been enough to choke those following. No record exists of the interval of march, but there must have been considerable separation between elements just to allow the dust of passage to settle.

Beyond Gaza we are told of another march to the city of Yehem, farther north. It was here that Thutmoses III called a final rest for his forces and held his council of war. Based on records of the campaign, this was a time to set strategy, hash out any tactical disagreements and configure the army for movement to contact.

The ruler of Megiddo certainly knew the Egyptians were coming. Thutmoses III encountered an enemy skirmish group immediately upon exiting the Aruna Pass. The skirmish group was not large, and dispersed quickly. It may have been something along the lines of a general outpost, such as is used in modern defensive action to warn of the precise route taken by the enemy and to engage in harassing action to serve notice that the advance would be opposed.

The main forces of Megiddo arrayed themselves in front of the city, in a full encampment preparatory to a large, set-piece battle. Superior Egyptian forces overwhelmed them. The surviving soldiers from the forces of Megiddo escaped behind the walls of the city. This was possible, we are told, because the Egyptians paused to loot the enemy encampment, much to the displeasure of the Pharaoh. After a protracted siege, the city fell to the Egyptians. Notable among the Egyptian records of capture were 924 chariots, 2,041 horses, a number of enemy soldiers taken as slaves or to be conscripted into the Egyptian force and a harvest of just over 140,000 cubic feet of grain.

The precise disposition of the spoils of victory is not recorded, however under Egyptian tradition all bounty flowed from and therefore belonged to the Gods. There would be some sort of presentation ceremony, probably at the temple of the main God Amun. Slaves, horses and chariots might have been brought before the temple, but the quantity of grain far exceeded the expedition's transport capability. It was likely divided among provisions for garrisons left in the conquered area and rations for the main expedition's return to Egypt, with the sizable remainder being shuttled back to Egypt over time to replenish reserves used to launch the expedition and to build up the stocks needed both to insure against poor crops and to launch future campaigns.

Megiddo was the first of Thutmoses III's campaigns, and may have been the most critical in consolidating the Egyptian Empire's holdings in Canaan. Under Egyptian protocol, once key locations were seized a son of the local ruler was taken back to Egypt to be educated in Egyptian ways and later returned to rule as the Pharaoh's representative. Archaeological excavation has established a strong Egyptian cultural influence in Late Bronze Age Canaan, suggesting that this consolidation strategy was effective.

Thutmoses III campaigned throughout the remainder of his reign, conquering and consolidating city-states along the Eastern Mediterranean coast and ranging inland as he went. Each campaign was built on the success of the last, with each producing additional friendly outposts which could be relied on for logistical support. Trade and espionage capability expanded in proportion. His furthest reach was an expedition into the Kingdom of Mitanni, which entailed building boats on the Mediterranean coast and hauling them overland to cross the Euphrates.

Thutmoses III's ability to mount extended campaigns year after year derived in large part from the structure of the Egyptian system of governance. The fact that the country was split into Nomes, each with its own administration, overseen on a national basis by the Vizier, allowed the Pharaoh to be absent for long periods without disruption of the country's economic or administrative functions.

While Thutmoses III's expansion and consolidation of the Egyptian Empire was a stunning achievement it was, like any venture involving significant reward, a high risk undertaking. Failure at any point could have meant the loss or crippling of a major expeditionary force with significant consequences for the defense of not only the empire, but the nation of Egypt itself.

Thutmoses III never suffered stalemate, but successor Pharaohs would not always be so fortunate. Imperial ambition was not limited to Egypt.

HITTITE IMPERIAL EXPANSION

THE EGYPTIAN IMPERIAL EXPANSION UNDER Thutmoses III was assisted in part by geography. The nation of Egypt is guarded for most of its length by deserts on the east and west. Security forces were required only to protect Egyptian Imperial interests in Nubia to the south and to guard against Libyan incursion into the western Nile Delta. The remainder of the army could be dedicated to Thutmoses III's campaigns of conquest. The Hittites were not as fortunate. During the period of Egyptian Imperial expansion, they were fighting on several fronts under a succession of rulers.

Between the Hittites and the Black Sea, not far north of the Hittite capitol of Hattusas, lay the domain of the troublesome Kaska tribes. The Hittites had to maintain a series of strong points and constantly patrol the border against incursion. This was a high maintenance activity that returned little beyond security. The Kaska would be-devil the Hittites for centuries.

The western portion of Anatolia, just across the Aegean Sea from the Mycenaean Empire, was the domain of Assuwa. Hittite archives indicate this was a confederation of twenty some city-states. Around 1430 BC Assuwa revolted against Hittite domination. Partial although inconclusive Hittite documents allude to Mycenaean (Ahhiyawan in Hittite parlance) involvement. There is some artifact support for this idea. A successful Hittite campaign quelled the revolt and a regent was installed to govern the region. Shortly afterward the regent revolted. A second campaign was required to break up the confederation.

Contemporary Hittite writing is silent as to commercial reasons for their campaigns. We can postulate that a Bronze Age empire would be hostage to the metal that gave it power. Access to copper and tin would be paramount considerations in devising imperial strategy. Primary targets were the Euphrates River trade routes in Northern Syria. The city-states there were rich prizes, but also strong militarily. In the early years of Hittite expansion, this meant alliance with the powerful kingdom of Aleppo.

To the east lay the hostile kingdom of the Mitanni, known to the Hittites as *Rulers of the Land of Hurri*. On the Hittite-Mitanni border lay a major source of copper. The Mitanni themselves seem to have been a military and/or administrative elite of Indo-European extraction who came to dominate the Hurrian kingdom and other local fiefdoms. Their capitol, Washukanni, is among the major Bronze Age cities for which archaeologists are still searching. The Mitanni were known in their time for a military corps referred to as *maryannu*, who were by contemporary reputation the best charioteers in the region. The presence of an ambitious and capable military state on their economically critical eastern frontier absorbed considerable Hittite resources.

Prior to 1400 BC the Hittite imperial situation was fluid. At one point the capitol, Hattusas, was taken and burned, possibly by the Kaska. Loss of the imperial capitol might seem to spell the end of the Empire, but the city appears to have been more an administrative center than a vital part of the imperial infra-structure. A similar episode occurred during the War of 1812 AD when the British burned the American capitol of Washington. The American government simply set up shop elsewhere when Washington was no longer viable. The Hittites, in their time, did likewise.

The Hittite Imperial Period, generally called the New Kingdom, not to be confused with the Egyptian New Kingdom, began around 1400 BC. The beginning of the period marked a low point in Hittite imperial prospects. The Mitanni had formed an alliance with Egypt, marrying one of the King's daughters off to the Egyptian Pharaoh Thutmoses IV. With the Egyptians to the south, the Mitanni to the east, the Kaska to the north and the Aegean and Mediterranean Seas and ultimately the Mycenaeans to the east, the Hittites were effectively hemmed in.

The Hittite king Tudhaliyas III, who ascended to power at the beginning of the New Kingdom, took on the job of consolidating the Hittite holdings within the boundaries established by external forces.

He was able by a combination of campaign and diplomacy to quell a number of internal revolts. He installed capable regents to forestall future difficulties and managed to placate some of the more restive city-states within the Empire. Some turmoil followed the reign of Tudhaliyas III, mainly in the form of power struggles that did not alter the shape or character of the Empire. The situation stabilized with the ascension of Suppiluliumas I.

Suppiluliumas I was an ambitious leader who had the good fortune to come to power at an auspicious time. The exact dates of his reign are still debated, but he is known to have ruled during the middle of the 14th Century BC. Roughly simultaneous events outside the Empire opened new opportunities for Hittite expansion. In 1360 BC the Assyrians, a growing Mesopotamian power, expelled the Mitanni, who had ruled their lands for decades. The Mitanni were engaged on two fronts, facing the Assyrians as well as the Hittites.

The Egyptian allies of the Mitanni were engaged by a major internal event. The Egyptian priesthood, representing a pantheon of gods, had been gaining power and amassing treasure through land ownership and mandatory offerings. The gain of any one sect was the losses of all the others. Their combined gains were the Pharaoh's losses. If the wealth and power of the nation continued to be split among quarrelsome religious factions, eventually the country would become ungovernable.

Pharaoh Amenhotep IV, who came to power in 1353 BC, devised a unique solution. He established a single national religion devoted to the sun disk Aten, banned all other religions and confiscated their wealth. To ensure that no priesthood arose under the new order, he forbade prayer directly to Aten. Instead he named himself Akhenaten and required that all prayer be directed to him as the earthly representative of Aten. He in turn would pray to the god on behalf of his supplicants. Needless to say, this did not go down well with the established priesthood. Akhenaten had his hands full enforcing his edicts. Pleas from his generals in Canaan went unheeded. Defense of the Asian Empire and the alliance with the Mitanni became secondary to Egyptian national concerns.

Suppiluliumas I was quick to take advantage of his situation. He continued the internal consolidation of the existing Hittite Empire and stiffened the defenses of Hattusas, expanding the city to the form in which it can be seen today. He then turned his attention to the newly vulnerable kingdom of Mitanni. After a failed expedition through the rugged Taurus Mountains, he was able to prosecute a successful campaign along the Euphrates River and sack the Mitanni capitol.

Most other cities in the region submitted rather than face the same fate. The city of Carchemish, which controlled a major crossing of the Euphrates, appears to have remained relatively independent for a time. The situation in the East was stable, if not ideal. Suppiluliumas I was in a position to turn his attention to the South and Syria. Kadesh, a key Syrian city whose king had figured in the revolt against Egypt at Megiddo, put up some resistance but capitulated. Surviving treaties from the period establish that the Hittite dominion spread widely through what had been the northern portion of the Egyptian Empire.

Suppiluliumas I's expansion of the Hittite borders was not a linear chronological progression. Trouble erupted fairly soon in Mitanni, when the King was assassinated and his successor refused to recognize Hittite control. Suppiluliumas I responded with a follow-up campaign in which he conquered Carchemish and installed a vassal ruler for the Mitanni kingdom. This was the height of the Hittite Empire, with the southernmost of its conquests coming at the expense of the Egyptian Empire and bringing the southern border approximately to the Litani River, near the southern border of modern Lebanon.

By that time Egypt had recovered from its internal struggles following the death of the Pharaoh Akhenaten. His son, Pharaoh Tutankhaten, renamed himself Tutankhamun to recognize the traditional chief god of Egypt. Amarna, the newly built city of Aten, the Sun disk, was abandoned. This produced a bonanza for modern scholars. The trove of official documents left behind, collectively known as the *Amarna Letters*, has provided a broad and detailed insight into both the diplomatic and political activity of the Eastern Mediterranean region between specific dates in the Late Bronze Age.

Political intrigue following the death of Tutankhamun brought the only known attempt to consolidate the Egyptian and Hittite Empires. Anksanamun, the widowed sister-bride of Tutankhamun, contacted the Hittites following the death of her husband and asked that a Hittite prince be provided to marry her and share the throne of Egypt. Suppululiumas I was happy to oblige, but the intended groom never reached Egypt. Historians suspect foul play at the instigation of either Ai, the elderly Vizier who succeeded Tutankamun as Pharaoh, or Horemheb, the general who succeeded Ai.

Suppululiumas I died as the result of an epidemic, reportedly carried by captured Egyptian soldiers. This is noteworthy not so much for the event as for its aftermath. In the Late Bronze Age, rampant disease was considered the wrath of the gods. In Suppululiumas I's case, large scale offerings known today as the *Plague Prayers* were made in propitiation.

The same activity is seen in Homer's *Iliad,* where pestilence is viewed as the arrows of Apollo and offerings are made at his altar. The Egyptians had their own goddess of plagues and epidemics, Sekhmet, whom they propitiated when such misfortunes befell them. The absence of such activity on a widespread basis at the time of the simultaneous collapse of the three Eastern Mediterranean Empires more than a century later argues persuasively that the collapse was not caused by a virus, as has been suggested.

Events following the death of Suppululiumas I brought the Hittite throne into the hands of an inexperienced ruler, Mursilis II. The Assyrians in Mesopotamia seized a small border kingdom in what was left of Mitanni and established a frontier with the Hittites in Northern Syria. Revolt broke out in Southern Anatolia and additional pressures came from the perennially troublesome Kaska tribes to the north. These were scarcely contained when revolt broke out after the death of the King of Carchemish, supported by both the Egyptians and Assyrians. Mursilis II was able to suppress this action and at his death left a relatively secure Empire to his successor Muwatallis II. External threats remained, notably to the south.

Pharaoh Seti I, who came to the throne in Egypt in the closing years of the 14th Century BC, was eager to repossess territories seized by the Hittites during the period when they enjoyed comparative strength. Campaigns were launched which enjoyed limited success in the Amurru region at the southern reaches of the Hittite Empire.

Even though border hostilities simmered, the Late Bronze Age empires of the Egyptians, the Hittites and the Mycenaeans had, by 1300 BC, achieved a stable balance of power. Each was politically and militarily secure within its own dominion. Documents show a robust flow of diplomatic activity.

Dwarfing these aspects of empire in importance was the economic activity necessary to support a technically sophisticated and highly organized civilization. Serial conquest could amass an empire but could not sustain it. Underpinning the three Eastern Mediterranean Empires was a trade network that sourced raw materials and distributed finished goods from England to India, Sub-Saharan Africa to Northern Europe. The geographic center of this trade was the Hittite Empire.

SHIPWRECK AT ULUBURUN

TRADING ACTIVITY AMONG THE EASTERN Mediterranean Empires has been known to scholars for more than a century. The knowledge was based on random mention in contemporary writing and archaeological discoveries of one empire's products in the sphere of another. These offered no insight into the volume involved or the importance of trade to the participating empires. The scope and scale of economic interdependence among the empires have recently become evident. It was the Eastern Mediterranean itself, lying adjacent to all three empires that helped to create and now is beginning to reveal this interdependence.

Archaeology has provided a window into the extent of imperial trade through the meticulous excavation of a ship wreck found off the coastal town of Uluburun in Turkey. Shipwrecks are unique in that they provide a perfect snapshot in time, isolated from contamination by either past or subsequent events. The Uluburun wreck has been dated to approximately 1300 BC. This dating was cross-referenced by four different methods. Pottery found on board allowed seriation. The surviving wooden structure was able to support dendrochronology, producing an exact date of 1305 BC for the felling of trees used in construction. Radiocarbon dating could be used on plant material. A piece of jewelry with the scarab of Queen Nefertiti permitted reference to the established Egyptian King List.

The ship's cargo was a mix of loads revealing the broad scope of goods traded at the time. There were ten tons of unusually pure copper. The copper ingots showed signs of multiple pours, which could indicate refining. The low level of impurities made it impossible to determine the source of the metal. There was one ton of tin, the other component of bronze. This was chemically degraded to the point where it also could not be identified as to source. There were hippopotamus teeth from Egypt, ebony from Nubia (probably by way of Egypt), elephant ivory from either India or Sub-Saharan Africa, ingots of glass from Mesopotamia and jars and pottery from Canaan and Cyprus. The pottery was used in part to ship a range of comestibles. Whatever enmity might have existed between empires and kingdoms, they apparently did not let it get in the way of business.

The cedar used in the construction of the ship was native to Lebanon, Southern Turkey and Cyprus. The vessel may have been a product of the Canaanite ship building industry. Canaan was a center of trade, so the operators may also have been Canaanite, although the ship could have been sold or chartered to other operators. Artifacts suggest that there was some Mycenaean presence on board. We do not know whether they were passengers, crew or supercargo. While we do not know the origin or destination of the ship, the wreck and its context lead us to an important conclusion about the scale of Late Bronze Age economic activity and infrastructure in the Eastern Mediterranean.

When the wreck was first explored, the theory was put forth that the rich cargo indicated an important vessel, perhaps even an imperial flag ship. This is clearly not the case. Fresco representations on the Minoan (Mycenaean) island of Thera show a fleet of ships of various sizes. Based on a comparison of a count of rowing stations on both the wreck and the Thera fresco, the Uluburun wreck, about fifty feet long, was a typical small-to-medium sized vessel for the times. Larger ships were nothing new to the region. More than 1,000 years earlier the building of the great Egyptian pyramids at Giza required the import of vast quantities of material over water. Excavation at a contemporary seaport on the Red Sea found the remains of boats 80 feet in length.

The Uluburun cargo includes fresh flora from Crete which could only have been loaded for a winter voyage. Even in later Roman times the Mediterranean was considered extremely dangerous to sail in the storm season from November to March. That Late Bronze Age merchant ships accepted this challenge indicates that year round traffic was necessary to sustain the empires of the time. Total annual Eastern Mediterranean sea trade would have been exponentially larger than the cargo of the Uluburun wreck, at least in the tens of thousands of tons.

The presence of cargo from the Island of Crete establishes that the wreck was not simply a coaster, visiting ports of call without ever venturing out of sight of land. Trade with Crete required an open-sea transit without reference to landmarks or hope of rescue in the event of catastrophe. The same is true of copper-rich Cyprus and of Thera, where the fleet fresco was found in the ruined town of Akrotiri overlooking what would have been, prior to the Santorini eruption, a large harbor. The fact that these islands enjoyed trade based economies establishes a level of maritime sophistication that supported routine voyages over open water.

Open sea transit has several requirements; seaworthy vessels, motive power and means of navigation. The fact that Crete, Cyprus and Thera were settled is adequate testimony to the long-standing availability of seaworthy vessels. Motive power was available from three sources; ocean currents, wind and oarsmen. Primary currents run clockwise as a result of the Earth's rotation. In the Eastern Mediterranean, this is advantageous for a north to south voyage. Sailors can tap into the planet's natural kinetic energy and make steady progress with minimal effort. South to north travel was also possible due to the prevailing wind. Chronic low atmospheric pressure in the area is over Anatolia. This means the prevailing winds flow from South to North (actually Southeast to Northwest) in the Eastern Mediterranean. Neither solution was perfect, and ships of the time were fitted with rowing stations in proportion to their length.

Navigation would have been more daunting. There are two primary methods of determining position. The first is dead reckoning. The method is to start in a known direction from a known position and use the speed of travel and elapsed time to compute the new position. The second method is resection. In the simplest terms, the method is to sight the angle to two known reference points to determine the current position. This is sometimes called triangulation, since it the two reference points and the navigator's location form the points of a triangle.

Dead reckoning would have been particularly difficult for open sea transit in the Late Bronze Age. Direction finding by use of the magnetic compass is not known to be in common use before the 14th Century AD, and significant over-water distances must account for the curvature of the Earth. There is no evidence that spherical trigonometry was practiced in the Late Bronze Age.

Resection was practical, although at a crude level. Since the voyagers were out of sight of land, the horizon was at exact sea level. This meant that latitude could be measured either as the angle of the sun at its highest point, or the angular relationship to the North Star. Any observed difference from the desired reading gives both the direction and magnitude of course correction required. Longitude is more complex, but can be approximated with the use of accurate star charts. Stars are fixed in relation to the Earth; their apparent movement across the sky is the result of the planet's daily rotation and its annual revolution around the sun. For a specific longitude, date and time, reference stars have a specific angular relationship.

Star tables and azimuth measuring devices are known to have existed in the Late Bronze Age. The concepts of latitude and longitude were documented in common usage by 150 AD. Ptolemy's world atlas, published in that year, contained coordinates for enough locations to suggest that the concept had been in place long before his time. Even without a specific world grid, the angular relationships with the sun and stars would have allowed position to be reckoned in much the same way.

The exact maritime navigation tools and techniques of the Late Bronze Age are not documented and remain to be discovered. A later shipwreck off the Island of Antikythera yielded a highly sophisticated mechanical device capable of establishing astronomical relationships, including the complex 18 year cycle of the moon.

Astronomical navigation was practiced by centuries of mariners. In a sea bordered by rocky coasts and swept by violent storms it could be dangerously imprecise. Records of later civilizations worldwide report significant navigation related losses prior to the late 18th Century AD development of the sextant and chronometer to closely reckon longitude. In one notorious incident in the early 18th Century AD, flawed navigation led to the wreck of a British naval fleet, with the loss of some 2,000 lives.

Large scale sea trade required an infrastructure of ship building and repair facilities to replace and mitigate inevitable losses. Also required was a network of secure harbors fed by overland routes capable of providing wide scale distribution of goods from coastal centers. Only a stable empire with a strong military could build and secure this sort of infrastructure. The Empires depended on a robust trade network to underpin their economies and the trade network depended on the Empires to provide a secure environment in which to operate.

Given the substantial capital investment, the complexity of navigation and the risk of storms and pirates, it is reasonable to ask why the Late Bronze Age Empires would rely on sea trade for any destinations but isolated islands like Crete and Cyprus. Why not simply rely on land caravans to conduct trade? The answer is money. According to later estimates by the Romans, who developed by far the most advanced road network of any ancient empire, it was up to twenty times cheaper to transport goods by sea than by land. In order for the Late Bronze Age Empires to function at the level they did without prohibitive costs, it was essential to use the Eastern Mediterranean as the primary trade corridor.

The available evidence strongly suggests that this is exactly what they did. The sophistication of the Uluburun ship could not have evolved without long term, large scale ship-building experience. The Thera fresco testifies to a significant fleet moored at a relatively small island. One of the Stela in the burial place of Pharaoh Amenhotep III is strongly suggestive of the itinerary of a significant sea voyage with ports of call in both the Hittite and Mycenaean Empires.

The growth of large cites at the coastal terminus of land trade routes in Canaan is further evidence of extensive sea trade as an extension of land commerce. Major cities of the Mycenaean Empire were sited on or near the coast. The Aegean Islands could be reached only by sea. Surviving tales of Mycenaean times revolve around sea voyages and trade. Legend has the Trojan War arising from the events of a sea trading expedition from Troy to the Achaean city of Sparta.

The careful listing of fleets transporting the Achaean (Mycenaean) invasion force in the *Iliad* may be lore, but it indicates that later societies accepted as fact the idea that each city of the Achaean Confederation possessed a significant number of ships, and that number was relative to the wealth and power of the city. Certainly the cities would not have had ships just lying about. If they existed, they would have been used in trade. Also accepted as fact was the notion that they made the transit across the Aegean to Anatolia. They were open-sea vessels.

Further confirmation of the importance of sea trade to the Mycenaeans comes from the *Voyage of Argo,* also lore in roughly the same class as the *Iliad.* When the Achaeans wanted to open new trade possibilities, they built and launched the Argo rather than explore land routes. Portions of the *Voyage of Argo* have been replicated in modern times, proving both the practicality of the voyage and the rigors of Late Bronze Age seafaring.

It was not only by accident of geography that the Late Bronze Age Empires of the Eastern Mediterranean became the hub of an international trade network stretching into India, Africa, Mesopotamia and Europe. They were, by virtue of location, able to provide distribution centers for wide area trade and, by virtue of sophistication, able to provide a demand for raw materials in industrial quantities and, by virtue of strength, able to provide the secure infrastructure necessary to maintain the necessary routes and facilities. Trade in turn sustained the Empires. The scale of monumental architecture and societal organization achieved by the Empires would not have been possible without a corresponding scale of economic activity.

While a mutually enriching system of trade and empire offered great advantages, it rested on a precarious balance. Large scale trade could not prosper without the voracious appetites and secure environments of the great Empires. Cooperation across the participating empires was essential. If the strength of any one element faltered, it could begin an accelerating spiral of events that could end in catastrophic collapse.

In 1300 BC the system was robust. External forces were held at bay by a combination of military force and a complex of alliances. The imperial business model, however, was built on expansion. With empires and ambitious kingdoms abutting each other, there was no room to expand. Pressures were mounting that would pit the great Empires against each other in spite of their economic interdependence.

Both the emboldened Egyptians and the entrenched Hittites harbored plans for expansion at the other's expense, casting covetous eyes once again on long contested border regions. Both Empires must have been aware of the prevailing interdependence in trade, but it is likely each saw no loss in overall prosperity if they took control of territory they saw as rightfully theirs anyway. After all, the current situation had grown out of centuries of conflict. Unlike past see-saw shifts in borders, which had come about as a result of alternating periods of strength and weakness, both combatants had at their disposal significant military power and leaders willing and able to focus it to further their imperial ambitions in the land that is modern day Lebanon and Syria.

THE BATTLE OF KADESH

I~N April of 1274~ BC Pharaoh Ramses II mounted a massive military expedition with the objective of expanding Egypt's Asiatic Empire northward at Hittite expense. Previous forays by his father, Seti I, had met with success in the Amurru region, the southern portion of modern Lebanon, and resulted in the capture of the key city of Kadesh in southern Syria. The Hittites subsequently re-took Kadesh. In 1274 BC Kadesh was the first objective on Ramses II's northward march. The Hittite King Muwatallis II was equally ambitious. He was already in the field with a numerically superior force, determined to reverse the earlier Egyptian successes and expand his own empire southward at Egyptian expense.

The Hittites' expeditionary force is cited in contemporary documents as 37,000 infantry and 3,500 chariots. The infantry was composed of Hittite regular troops and troops levied from vassal states, referred to in contemporary documents as *teher*. Egyptian documents provide a laundry list of Hittite allies, including troops from the kingdom of Mitanni; the Anatolian kingdoms of Azwara, Arawana, Pitasa, Dardania, Mysia, Karkisa, Wilusa and Lycia; and the Syrian kingdoms of Carchemish, Ugarit and Aleppo. Several other names in the Egyptian records are not known and may refer to mercenary groups rather than vassal states. Additional mercenary elements appear to have been hired from the Shasu, local barbaric nomads.

Ramses II staged four regular Egyptian divisions northward from the border garrison at Sile and a fifth group eastward from the Mediterranean coast. Egyptian records cite the north bound force in order of march as the Amun, Re, Seth and Ptah divisions. These were comprised of Egyptian troops augmented by sizeable contingents of mercenaries. Frequently mentioned among the mercenaries are the

Sherden, sea-borne raiders who were defeated by Ramses II in 1278 BC and subsequently used to augment the Egyptian military. Nothing is written of their origins, but pictorial representations show body armor similar to Mycenaean corselets. Egyptian scribes also refer to Dardanian allies (a name familiar from Homer's *Iliad*) and to the Peleset (Philistines), whom we will encounter later.

The group staged eastward from the coast is given the name Na'arm. The exact composition is not known. Since Na'arm is a Canaanite word, the most promising theory is that it consisted of an Egyptian command cadre and troops levied from vassal states. Ramses II's primary maneuver element appears to have been the division. The Na'arm group was of sufficient size to help turn the tide of battle against a powerful Hittite force. It is reasonable to postulate that the group was of division size.

Each Egyptian division numbered 5,000 infantry. Chariot strength can be estimated at between 2,500 and 3,500 vehicles. This gives a total Egyptian battle strength of at least 30,000 men. This in turn meant a combined force of approximately 80,000 combatants, Hittite and Egyptian. Supporting labor would have numbered at least an additional 20,000. The logistics train would have consisted mostly of human packers. The design of a collar that allowed horses to pull heavy loads without choking was not developed until the 9th Century AD. In total, some 100,000 men were converging on the city of Kadesh, on the river Orontes, an area that presented significant challenges for large scale encampment and maneuver.

While we know something of Thutmoses III's campaign against Megiddo, Kadesh is the earliest ancient battle for which we have any detailed description of the actual engagement. Well-meaning historians have embellished the contemporary accounts with faux-three dimensional computer renderings, precise combatant positioning and sequences of maneuver. The fact is that our information about the actual battle remains sketchy. No Hittite narrative of the battle has yet been discovered. All we have from their perspective is reference from related documents. The Egyptian narrative, which we are obliged to follow, is clearly intended to serve propaganda purposes.

The engagement was fought more than three thousand years ago. Erosion and accretion make terrain features subject to revision over that length of time. The contemporary course of the Orontes is not known with any precision. There is some suggestion that the river was partially re-channeled to form a moat around the city, but this has not been established. The general surroundings of the city can be inferred from available information. Egyptian records refer to passage through the Labni Wood, indicating that forestation was common in the area. The fact that a large Hittite army went undiscovered by whatever preliminary scouting the Egyptian force did suggests that to the North and East of the city vegetation was thick enough and terrain erose enough to offer concealment.

The city itself would have been close enough to the river to guarantee a steady supply of water but would not have been built in the flood plain. From this we can infer considerable vertical relief in the immediate area of the river, limiting the number of crossing points. In addition, April was flood season, resulting in difficult crossing even where possible. An abundance of fresh water in early spring would have promoted widespread growth of low vegetation, a further hindrance to military maneuver on any scale. Kadesh was destroyed only a century or so after the battle. Its remains are thought to be in a lower layer of a ruin mound, or tell, in the orchard country of southern Syria. The site has not been excavated so we do not have physical evidence of the nature or extent of the city's fortifications and are not able to validate their reported role in the battle.

Approaching from the south, the main Egyptian force would have to cross the River Orontes to reach the city. This would have been a perilous undertaking with a large Hittite force known to be in the area. The crossing was initiated by what appeared to be a fortuitous bit of intelligence. The Egyptians encountered two nomads, who reported that the Hittite force was still well to the north of Kadesh. Ramses II ordered his main force across the Orontes, going himself with the leading Amun Division to set up his headquarters in an area thought by modern historians to be to the north and west of the city.

This would be the base from which he would stage operations against the city. It also may have been a pre-arranged rendezvous point with the Na'arm group arriving from the coast. The Egyptians had campaigned extensively in the area and knew both the available routes of march and times required for passage, so that closely coordinated movement was possible. A timely rendezvous may have been part of Ramses II's motivation to move the four divisions accompanying him north of the river.

Crossing the Orontes with an army of more than 30,000 men accompanied by animals, vehicles and supplies was not something that could be accomplished quickly. This fact was exploited by the Hittite commander. Muwatallis II had provided the Egyptians with their fortuitous intelligence. His forces were in fact not far to the north and east of Kadesh, lying in wait for the Egyptians.

Muwatallis II allowed Ramses II to cross the river with the Amun division unmolested. When the second of Ramses II's subordinate commands, the Re Division, crossed the river, Muwatallis II's chariot forces fell on them. Many historians have been puzzled by this facet of the battle. They question how Muwatallis II could have hidden an army numbering more than 40,000 and then clandestinely maneuvered an assault force said to be 2,500 chariots into position to attack the Re Division. Upon close inspection of the situation, this becomes less improbable.

First, the King of Kadesh was expected to put up resistance, and would have forces in the area, including three man Asiatic chariots built on the Hittite model. Muwatallis II did not have to conceal the presence of an army, merely its size. This was made easier by the fact that he withheld the majority of his infantry, which was by far the largest component of his expedition. Second, the Re Division's order of march would not have been an unbroken line of troops, but rather a staggered file of small units spread out over miles as they made their way toward Ramses II's camp. This was an administrative march, not a tactical movement to contact such as Thutmoses III's much earlier approach to Megiddo through the Aruna Pass. Commanders would maintain unit separation to keep following units from choking on the dust of those ahead. Also, various types of units would cross the Orontes at different rates. This would require Muwatallis II to break his chariot assault force into corresponding small units.

Since the King of Kadesh was likely to be actively reconnoitering, the Egyptian commanders, focused on the considerable challenges of moving a large force across the river, may have interpreted reports of chariot units moving in the vicinity of the Re Division's line of march as simply multiple sightings of the same insignificant scouting or screening from the city. In any event, Muwatallis II' forces did attack, inflicting significant damage. Precise casualty figures are not known, but the Re Division was scattered and rendered combat ineffective.

The Hittites had succeeded in cutting Ramses II's force in two, with Ramses II and the Amun Division on one side of the Orontes and vulnerable while his two remaining intact divisions were on the other side, unable to provide timely reinforcement. To aid in visualizing the situation, a diagram of force disposition is included at the end of this chapter. The diagram is in block form to avoid any spurious presentation of scale, topography or vegetation.

Muwatallis II pressed his apparent advantage with an attack on Ramses II's camp. A mobile archery capability allowed the Hittites to deliver as many as 25,000 accurately placed arrows in a short space of time. The Amun division was unable to mount an effective defense of the camp and withdrew.

Muwatallis II's decision to attack with only chariot forces, probably accompanied by minimal infantry to consolidate gains, may have been due in part to terrain, timing and disposition considerations. Ramses II's encampment site would have been chosen to accommodate an army of over 40,000, including support troops and logistics train. Applying the standard ratio of one acre of campground required for every one hundred soldiers, this would indicate an area of more than 400 acres or the good part of a square mile of open ground. The Amun Division would have been spread thin securing and preparing an encampment for a population eight times its size. A force of 2,500 chariots attacking before any significant defense works could be put in place would have a considerable tactical advantage.

In addition, Muwatallis II knew the Na'arm division had staged from the coast to join the Egyptian force. It would have been impossible to move that size element without attracting the attention of the Hittite espionage network. It is possible that he was informed as to the scheduled time of arrival of the Na'arm group and was pressing his attack to destroy the Egyptian force before reinforcements became available.

Muwatallis II was unable to follow up the advantage he gained by displacing the Amun division and defeating the Re Division. The Hittites became bogged down in looting the Egyptian camp. Records from centuries of Egyptian campaigns in the area suggest that much battlefield loot was in the form of horses and captured soldiers. Since both categories are mobile, prompt scavenging of the battlefield was necessary. The wealth associated with a Pharaoh's encampment may have provided additional incentive to vassal state commanders and mercenaries with no particular loyalty to the Hittite elite.

The delay allowed Ramses II to organize his forces, consisting at least of the Amun Division and whatever stragglers remained from the Re Division. At this point the narrative focuses on the Pharaoh's personal heroics. It is vague as to the timing of the arrival of the Na'arm group. According to Egyptian accounts the group did participate in the battle at some point. Given the length of a division sized column, at least the lead elements of the Na'arm group must have arrived in time to participate in Ramses II's initial counter-attack. The Egyptians dislodged the Hittite forces from their positions. Muwatallis II responded by committing his reserve of 1,000 chariots to the battle.

By this time the Egyptian Seth Division had crossed the Orontes, and Ramses II pressed his numerical advantage. The Hittite chariot group was driven in some disarray to a point on the Orontes where there was no ford available. Egyptian accounts have chariot crews swimming as fast as crocodiles, but substantial allowance must be made for hyperbole. Some modern accounts have faster and lighter two man Egyptian chariots overtaking and destroying the heavier fleeing Hittite three man vehicles. This is pure invention. No scientific performance comparison has ever been conducted between the two vehicle types, nor is one possible today. The physiology of horses has morphed dramatically in the intervening time. Egyptian horses of the 2nd Millennium BC more closely resembled asses than modern horses. Radar timing of a replica Egyptian chariot drawn by modern horses under suitably revised harness recorded a speed of twenty five miles per hour on flat ground. This would not have been sustainable over a rough battle field. The terrain dictated the speed of chariot movement and negated any Egyptian advantage that might have existed.

Vehicle speed aside, it is unlikely that Egyptian commanders would have permitted their valuable chariot forces to break ranks and dash off in headlong pursuit. This would have involved outrunning their protective infantry. It seems more likely that the Egyptians were able to remain organized and maintain pressure on the disorganized Hittite chariot force. The contemporary account has the Hittite survivors being pulled over the walls of Kadesh into the city. This would have been impossible in a hot pursuit scenario.

The situation at the City of Kadesh proper differed greatly from the battlefield at Ramses II's camp. Far from victory, the Egyptians had achieved only stalemate. The Hittite assault force, their chariots, had suffered significant attrition, but their massive infantry force had not yet engaged and were encamped at Kadesh. Four of Ramses II's five divisions had suffered battle losses. His early successes had left him too weak to further contest the issue. He withdrew his remaining army, leaving Kadesh in Hittite hands.

This outcome is particularly noteworthy because it calls into question the Late Bronze Age war fighting scenario put forth by many modern scholars. It has been widely written that Late Bronze Age imperial armies attacked with chariots followed by infantry to immediately exploit any breeches in enemy formations. The Hittite king Muwatallis II was an experienced field commander with able counsel from battle-hardened subordinates. He had ample opportunity to commit his main infantry force, both in the initial assault and at the point when he committed his chariot reserves. The fact that he elected not to do so suggests that disposition of forces in Late Bronze Age warfare was more complex than we currently understand.

Although Muwatallis II retained control of the city, he had lost his chariot assault force. He would have to wait to pursue his goal of recapturing territory in the Amurru region previously lost to the Egyptians. While the outcome at Kadesh is a critical piece in the puzzle of the fall of empire in the late 2nd Millennium BC, it is only the beginning of the story. The stalemate at Kadesh exacted a price that impaired both combatants and brought unforeseen consequences.

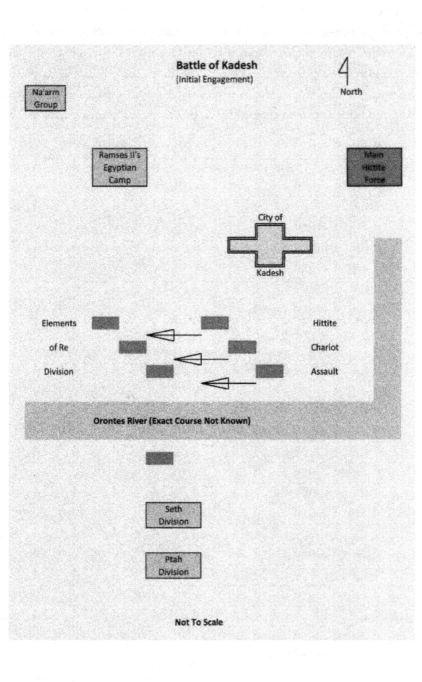

Battle of Kadesh
(Initial Engagement)

North

Na'arm Group

Ramses II's Egyptian Camp

Main Hittite Force

City of

Kadesh

Elements

of Re

Division

Hittite

Chariot

Assault

Orontes River (Exact Course Not Known)

Seth Division

Ptah Division

Not To Scale

THE COST OF KADESH

———— ⟡ ————

BEGINNING WITH SARGON THE BASIS of empire building was the investment of capital to gain access to resources through domination of existing states. Much of this investment manifested itself in establishing, maintaining and deploying a superior military force to first subdue opposing forces and then to secure conquest. The resources flowing from conquered provinces in excess of the cost of their administration would be reinvested in additional conquest or in the construction of infrastructure to enhance the efficiency of the existing realm. In modern jargon, this was the imperial business model.

The stalemate at Kadesh meant there would be no resource gain from the enterprise for either side. Setbacks in executing the imperial business model were not uncommon, but at Kadesh the impact of stalemate was magnified by the scale of the undertaking. The investments in the Kadesh campaign made by both the Egyptians and Hittites were astronomical. Since we have more records from the Egyptian side, we will focus on the cost of Ramses II's campaign first.

Ramses II's expedition to Kadesh was not an isolated foray. It was undertaken in his 5th regnal year as a continuation of earlier campaigns by both Ramses II and Seti I that re-took parts of the Ammuru region from the Hittites. Given the extensive espionage networks in place at the time, Ramses II was undoubtedly aware that the Hittites were preparing a large expeditionary force to reverse the recent Egyptian gains. An assault on the key Syrian city of Kadesh would require a massive army but, if successful, it would blunt the Hittite counter-offensive and produce enough immediate treasure and future flow of resources to justify the cost.

The size and composition of Ramses II's force determine the direct cost of the expedition. We know that four divisions, each containing

5,000 infantry staged from Sile. Another group, probably of division size staged from the Mediterranean coast. This establishes a core of 25,000 infantry. It has been suggested that the divisions may have been at less than full strength, with estimates of Egyptian infantry strength running from 10,000 to 15,000. These estimates are entirely theoretical, not supported by contemporary sources and run counter to logic. Control and re-supply of an infantry expedition requires a command and logistical infrastructure. Since the Egyptian divisions at Kadesh were cited as separate elements, we can infer a separate infrastructure for each division. 10,000 to 15,000 infantry could be accommodated within two or three divisions, reducing the required administrative overhead. The specific naming of five divisions in contemporary accounts argues persuasively for an infantry strength of 25,000.

Egyptian chariot forces are not specified. We do know that Hittite chariot strength was 3,500. Presumably Ramses II's spies would have provided a good estimate of Hittite strength. Ramses II would have striven to at least achieve parity in numbers. 3,500 chariots would require a crew total of 7,000, with support personnel of around 2,000.

The size of the logistics train is more difficult to estimate. One clue is contained in the visual representation of Ramses II's encampment. These clearly show oxen. Oxen were prized for strength rather than speed or endurance. Their nutritional requirements per mile travelled were high. They would have been used only when required to move the significant loads associated with a large logistics train. Even using a minimal estimate would bring the personnel count in Ramses II's force to at least 40,000.

Julius Caesar famously wrote that an army travels on its stomach. Logistical studies by the US Army following World War I indicated that a single soldier in the field requires a minimum of 3,000 calories of nutrition per day. This places Ramses II's food requirements at 120 million calories per day for his force of 40,000 personnel.

We can make a gross assumption that pack animals were used only for transport of non-consumable goods, while human porters carried the expedition's food. The underlying logic is that as the expedition progressed and meals were consumed, the load of food would diminish.

If animals were used to transport it, then the expedition would be burdened with the care and feeding of an increasing number of unladen animals. Human porters could be re-purposed to useful tasks such as local foraging and manual labor. Additional reduction in the logistics train could be achieved by having individual soldiers carry a portion of their own rations, and by prepositioning supplies at garrisons under Egyptian control along the route.

This would leave 7,000 chariot horses plus oxen and some donkeys to be fed. We can only estimate daily rations due to the fact that the Egyptian horse breed is extinct and no detailed contemporary records have been found. Modern animals provide a poor proxy due to differences in weight and musculature. As a gross approximation, each animal would require three times the daily nutrition of a man. Assuming a total of 7,500 animals, we can set the total food ration for animals at one half of the total for personnel, the calculation being the 3 times 7,500 equals an equivalent 22,500, rounded to 20,000. This provides a total daily nutrition requirement of 180 million calories per day for personnel and animals. To keep the estimated cost conservative the expedition's considerable hydration requirements are assumed to be taken, either by agreement or under threat, from local sources enroute.

Contemporary records indicate a march time of twenty one days from Sile to Kadesh. The Egyptian campaign to Kadesh was a two-way affair, with time spent at the battle site. The overall round trip would not have been less than 50 days. Conversion of calorie requirements to weight of food can provide only a gross estimate, since we do not know the calorie content of ancient foods. The majority of human food consumed (75% or more) was bread. A slice of modern bread weighing about 28 grams yields 70 calories. Without wading through the arithmetic of unit conversion, 180 million calories would equate to more than 150,000 pounds of bread, or 75 tons of modern bread equivalent per day. The 50 day round trip would call for 3,750 tons.

This estimate is arguably quite low, given that other foods would also be required, calorie counts are minimal for the activities undertaken and calorie values of ancient foods were probably lower than modern equivalents. Offsetting this are several factors. We do not know the distance or time of march for the Na'arm group. Nutrition requirements on the return trip would be reduced by battle losses. The notorious shortcomings in taste and quantity of battle rations throughout the centuries up to modern times suggest that actual food consumption might be less than ideal. It is common for soldiers to lose weight on campaign. The best we can hope to derive is an order of magnitude.

To place the burden of nutrition for the Kadesh campaign in perspective, monthly compensation for a well-placed civilian official of the time would include a little over 100 gallons of grain (5 khar in Egyptian parlance), which would be ample to feed a family of a dozen with some left over to trade for other goods. The grain consumed in the Kadesh campaign would have paid every official in all 42 nomes of Egypt several times over.

It is fair to ask if nutrition is a legitimate expense of the Kadesh expedition. After all, the personnel would have had to eat whether they were on campaign or not. The key determinant is that the personnel would have been performing other productive tasks within Egyptian society if they were not on campaign. Their nutrition would have been paid for by the fruits of those labors. If we are to estimate the profit or loss of Kadesh, we need to match the costs directly associated with the expedition against any reward gained as a result.

A cost clearly associated with the Kadesh campaign was the need to employ mercenary and allied forces to expand the Egyptian army. The Pharaoh not only had to counter the Hittite threat from the north but also to quell potential Nubian unrest in the south, hold Egypt's borders against Libyan incursion from the west and maintain internal security. Even allocating only one division and associated chariot forces to each of these tasks. The total size of Ramses II's army would have exceeded 60,000. Given a total Egyptian population of no more than 3 million, a conscript army would require that one in every fifty Egyptians be on active military service during this period. For comparison, the United States Army was legally limited to 500,000 during the time when it was fighting in both Iraq and Afghanistan. With a US population in excess of 300 million, this means only one in six hundred Americans were on active Army service, with the total military levy, including naval and air forces, only around one in three hundred, and serving on a paid volunteer basis.

In a pre-industrial economy such as ancient Egypt, where military-age males made up only a fraction of the population and were also the prime source of physical labor, a military overhead of one in fifty would have been out of the question, even after completion of the harvest. Large numbers of mercenaries had to be recruited to fill the infantry ranks, and the numbers made individual enlistment impractical. Rulers of the city-states and principalities capable of providing the required numbers and quality of experienced troops would have exacted the highest price available from the Pharaoh.

Egyptian records contain no specific information on where these mercenaries were sourced, beyond the already mentioned conscription of captured Sherden. The Sherden were apparently compensated through a system of resettlement. Tax records indicate that after their defeat the Sherden were spread throughout Egypt so that no district's population had more than a 5% Sherden component. The Sherden were given land to work and were required to pay taxes. This was an innovative solution that offered both economic incentive to the mercenaries and kept their families hostage to the Pharaoh, while bolstering the tax base. There is no indication, however, that this approach was applied to other mercenary groups.

The use of mercenaries by the Egyptians was traditional, but did represent a gamble. If Ramses II's campaign succeeded, they would be essential in guarding subjugated lands against rebellion and ensuring the safe transit of caravans through areas haunted by opportunistic barbarians. Payment from the proceeds of empire would ensure their continued loyalty. If the campaign failed, however, excess mercenaries would have to be paid off and dispersed quickly lest the Pharaoh find himself facing organized groups of armed and experienced fighters hungry for spoils. This would have added a dimension of immediacy to expenses in the aftermath of Kadesh.

The costs of mounting Ramses II's expedition and bringing it to Kadesh were immediate. The cost of the losses suffered at Kadesh lingered long after the battle, particularly in the chariot corps. Each chariot carried a crew of two, a driver and an archer, and was drawn by two horses. The drivers would have required considerable training in both the handling of the animals and vehicles. Horses also had to be matched and trained, a process consuming many months. Training was also required in formation maneuver. Experienced charioteers would have to be stripped from operational units to serve as trainers.

Archers required even more development in both skill and strengthening of the specific muscle groups necessary for repetitive, accurate launch of arrows from moving vehicles. Based on English records from the age of the long bow, it took seven years to develop a competent stationary archer, and continual practice to maintain proficiency. When firearms replaced archery, it wasn't because the musket offered better accuracy, range or penetration. In fact the musket was inferior in every category. The advantage of conversion to firearms was that a soldier with a musket could be trained in seven months, allowing rapid conscription and reducing the need for large and costly standing armies.

Ramses II did not enjoy this option. He had to make a considerable investment of time and resources to develop an army capable of undertaking the Kadesh expedition. While this army was not intended for exclusive use at Kadesh and its cost was not expected to be recouped only from the Kadesh expedition, a significant portion was lost or damaged at Kadesh. It is fair to attribute the cost of replacement of this portion to Kadesh.

Absent accurate figures on the Egyptian combat losses at Kadesh, it is not possible to estimate cost of replacement. If replacement did occur, it would have required considerable time during which the opportunity for conquest would be lost. It is not known from contemporary records to what extent Ramses II replaced losses or rebuilt his military. Future campaigns were conducted on a smaller scale, and it may be that he simply reorganized on a more cost-conscious basis. In either event the cost of the loss was the same, whether it was realized as an out-of-pocket replacement outlay or a cost of opportunity lost due to limits on the size of the army. The Hittites were able, over the next few years, to nibble away at Egyptian gains and recover effectively the entire Amurru region.

Taken in sum, even without precise estimates, the Egyptian expedition that culminated in the battle of Kadesh was a huge investment for which Ramses II saw no return. It can be argued that had Ramses II not fought the Hittites to stalemate at Kadesh they might have advanced southward beyond the Amurru region and seized more of Egypt's empire. Even so, manning the barricades at massive expense is not how the expansion-based imperial business model is designed to work.

The cost of the battle of Kadesh on the Hittite side is more difficult to estimate. Hittite infantry is recorded as 37,000, approximately three Hittites for every two Egyptians. The record of Hittite numerical superiority is supported by Ramses II's reluctance to engage the Hittite infantry even after overwhelming the Hittite chariot force. Hittite chariots are known to have carried three man crews as opposed to the Egyptian two man crews, preserving the same differential in the chariot corps.

An approximate three to two numerical Hittite manpower advantage suggests a daily ration requirement of 112 tons. The difficulty in estimating total cost for the Hittite expedition lies first in the fact that we don't know how far the expedition travelled. Contingents from Mitanni and the Anatolian kingdoms would have had a longer journey than the Egyptians. Without knowing the numerical make-up of the Hittite force, we cannot calculate an average journey length on which to base nutritional requirements. A second snag lies in the fact that some of the Hittite expedition did not return straightaway to their points of origin, but remained as garrison and to recapture territory that had been lost to recent Egyptian incursion. The best we can do is a general understanding that the Hittite nutritional requirements would have exceeded those of the Egyptians at least in proportion to relative force size.

While the Egyptians relied on mercenary forces, the Hittites may have drawn more heavily on vassal states and not required the same payroll outlay. The cost is equally onerous regardless of source. Resources provided by Hittite vassal states represented, as for the Egyptians, taxes that would otherwise have flowed to Hittite imperial coffers. It also limited future levies that could be made to replace decimated forces.

As with the Egyptians, the lingering cost of Kadesh came in the form of Hittite battle losses. Although we do not have precise casualty figures, we do know that Muwatallis II's assaults against Egyptian positions and lines of march were conducted largely by chariot forces. Successful Egyptian counter-attacks reasonably would have accounted for a good portion of the Hittite chariot force.

As with the Egyptians, the cost of this sort of loss is two-fold. First, there is a sizeable capital outlay to procure new chariots and horses. Second, there is a long period of training for chariot horses, drivers and archers. The time involved would be protracted by the fact that the Hittite military did not have leisure to rebuild and train. They had immediate operational requirements which would take priority. It is not a stretch to suggest that Muwatallis II's Kadesh campaign stripped the Empire of its reserves.

As expensive and unrewarding as the Battle of Kadesh proved to be, it did not bankrupt or otherwise cause the immediate collapse of the empires involved. In fact, the Mycenaean Empire did not participate in the clash at Kadesh, beyond the strong likelihood that some cities in the Empire provided mercenaries to one or both sides. The generally simultaneous collapse of the three empires, Egyptian, Hittite and Mycenaean, cannot be explained solely by the outcome or cost of Kadesh. The massive imperial confrontation at Kadesh did, however, place the highly interdependent Eastern Mediterranean world in a precarious position.

EGYPT AND THE EMPIRE
AFTER KADESH
⟨✑⟩

Ramses II's retreat to Egypt after Kadesh left him in a difficult position. The expedition had risked the nation's wealth, Ramses II's personal prestige and to some extent the concept of the Pharaoh as a divine being. After all, how could a living god fail to defeat a mere mortal like the King of the Hittites? Ramses II and his predecessors had returned proudly from earlier campaigns with captives and treasure to present at the temple of Amun. Ramses II made his way back from Kadesh with only a battered army. Given the size of the military contingent, news of the debacle at Kadesh was certain to spread widely. To retain his grip on power, Ramses II had to turn stalemate into triumph. To this requirement we are indebted for our knowledge of the engagement at Kadesh.

Ramses II undertook a massive propaganda offensive consisting of both monumental and practical architecture celebrating the Pharaoh's hard won victory. He commissioned a vast temple at Karnak and had the story of the battle immortalized on the panels of the walls. Both hieroglyphic narrative and pictorial renderings made much of his personal valor in rallying his beleaguered troops. The fact that no Hittites pursued the retreating Egyptians lent some credence to Ramses II's claim that he had defeated them. The tale was repeated in either full or abridged versions at Ramses II's mortuary temple and at temples in Abydos, Luxor and Abu Simbel.

Ramses II's reign following Kadesh was a period in which construction flourished. A new capital city was completed and named *House of Ramses, Great in Victory*, abbreviated today as Pi-Ramses. Ramses II's purpose went beyond propaganda. In the aftermath of Kadesh, Egyptian mentality turned from imperial expansion to defense of the Empire and the nation. The wholesale movement of the Egyptian capitol from Thebes, hundreds of miles up the Nile, was a massive undertaking. The new capitol city was built on an eastern branch of the Nile delta, near the old Hyksos capital of Avaris and closer to the Egyptian vassal states of Asia. From this location the Pharaoh's army could react quickly to threats from hostile Hittite forces to the north, and also to depredation by the Shasu, nomadic raiders who harried Canaan from the east. The move emphasizes how seriously the threat to the Asiatic Empire was taken.

Modern scholars knew of Pi-Ramses from extensive writings from the era, but the city had vanished. Locating Pi-Ramses was for decades the holy grail of Egyptian archaeology. It was finally discovered that the branch of the Nile on which it was built had begun to silt up about a century after its construction. Without access to the river that served as the nation's lifeline, Pi-Ramses was no longer viable as a capitol. The edifices and sculpture of the city had been moved to another location by a later Pharaoh. Examination of the stone works at the new location together with a picture of the original site developed with ground penetrating radar suggests a masterwork of urban planning and execution and helps to establish Ramses II's reign as a golden age for the nation of Egypt.

The situation in the Egyptian Empire declined as the nation prospered. The cost of the Kadesh expedition by itself was not insurmountable problem. As long as there was no famine, the surplus of Egyptian agriculture and taxes levied against the Empire over the next few years could replenish the nation's reserves with the general population none the wiser. The cost of Ramses II's ambitious construction was another matter. The only available source of the wealth required was the gold mines of Nubia. The amount of gold extracted was famous throughout the Middle East. The royal archives hold numerous diplomatic letters from allies trying to wheedle the precious metal from various pharaohs. While Nubian gold made Ramses II's golden age possible in Egypt, the situation understandably did not sit well with the Nubians.

Ramses II campaigned in Nubia, first to regain lost territory and expand Egypt's domain and subsequently to suppress multiple revolts.

Egypt was generally successful in maintaining the southern portion of the empire, but success came at a price. An ongoing military presence and requisite campaigns drew down resources that might have been used elsewhere.

The Asiatic Empire to the north and east were more problematic. Ramses II launched several campaigns into Canaan with the objective of pressing back the Hittites and gaining territory in Syria. He was able to prevail in several battles, but his gains proved ephemeral. As soon as he returned to Egypt or moved on to other campaigns, the captured territories reverted to their previous state. Eventually the Hittites re-took the territory lost to the earlier campaigns of Seti I and Ramses II. The stalemate at Kadesh expanded into an uneasy border stability. Although Ramses II never again mustered an expeditionary force of the size he took to Kadesh, he did maintain a large chariot and weapons manufacturing capability at Pi-Ramses.

Ramses II's strategy, either through his initiative or in response to the dictates of circumstance, seems to have been to field an army only large enough to secure the Asiatic Empire as it stood and hold as an option the capability to expand his military as a deterrent. This approach reduced his costs. In particular he would not have to pay large contingents of mercenaries unless and until they were actually needed. This was beneficial for Ramses II, but it left the mercenaries at loose ends with no source of revenue. A situation that would have repercussions.

Complicating Ramses II's military situation was pressure from the Libyans to the west. They had coveted parts of the Nile delta for centuries, and were growing aggressive. Ramses II campaigned in Libya, and was forced to maintain a considerable security presence on Egypt's western border. It became clear over time that imperial expansion by military means would not be practical.

Palace intrigue in the Hittite Empire did offer a brief flicker of hope. Ramses II for a time provided sanctuary to a pretender to the Hittite throne. This effort proved futile. Muwatallis II's' eventual successor to the Hittite throne, Hatusilis III was able to consolidate power. He had, however, inherited a weakened empire. The resulting difficulties led him to negotiate a peace treaty with the Egyptians in 1258 BC. This remarkable document, the first major peace treaty we know of, survives today. We are sure of its authenticity because the Egyptian and Hittite versions (both extant) are generally identical except for the prologue, in which each Empire announces that the treaty exists because they were victorious in imperial campaigns.

Provisions of the treaty called for trade relations, intermarriage among the royal families and mutual defense. While there was no specification of imperial boundaries, the treaty effectively ended the long-running border dispute between Egypt and the Hittites. This further reduced the Egyptian need to employ mercenaries. As before, costs saved by the Egyptians were revenues lost by the states providing the mercenaries. With large groups of fighters at loose ends, the long term stability of the Eastern Mediterranean empires grew less secure.

As Ramses II's reign wore on, the Hittite Empire grew progressively weaker. This manifested itself as requests for grain to stave off famine, rather than any opportunity to expand the Empire through military or diplomatic initiatives. In his later years Ramses II had to rely on proxy campaigns carried out by some of his many sons to defend Egypt and its holdings. Analysis of his mummy indicates that during this time he was crippled by arthritis. His dental problems were by then serious enough that he may have died of related infection. His reign, christened by modern scholars as Egypt's great age, did not end until 1213 BC, when he passed away at the age of 90.

Ramses II was succeeded by his son Merneptah. Merneptah's inheritance was an empire in decline. Circumstances forced him to campaign in areas previously seen as secure. A well known example is related in carvings of the so-called *Israel Stone* uncovered by Sir William Flinders Petrie in the late 19th Century AD. It is the first known Egyptian mention of an organized state in the area of Israel, and has been seized upon by Biblical scholars as evidence of an early Judean kingdom. The context of the mention may be more telling. It claims a successful campaign by Pharaoh Merneptah during which he raided and laid waste to several cities in Canaan in 1208 BC. The inscription closes with that statement that *everyone who was restless has been bound*; indicating that

Merneptah had been forced by circumstance to campaign in Canaan to pacify what was once a secure vassalage of the Egyptian Empire.

Additional difficulties arose in the west. Ramses II had established an outpost line beyond the settled western areas of the Nile Delta to provide early warning and combat capability in the event of Libyan incursion. This came during the reign of Merneptah. A large battle resulting in thousands of casualties was fought between the Egyptian army and a Libyan invasion reinforced by a large number of outsiders, sometimes referred to by scholars as allies of the Libyans but possibly mercenaries in the service of the Libyan king. Some were identified as Sherden, a group that had fought as mercenaries for Ramses II at Kadesh. The descendants of soldiers who had filled out the Egyptian Imperial ranks a few generations earlier were now arrayed to storm the Egyptian homeland.

Egyptian records list the outsiders as members of six distinct groups. As with the Sherden, the other five groups were specifically named. These names were probably enough to tell Egyptian readers of the period where the groups came from. Lacking this context, modern scholars have developed numerous theories but no consensus as to the sources of the Libyans' allies. This is not an insignificant question. The presence of a military element large and daring enough to threaten the borders of the Egyptian homeland shifted a critical dynamic. The Egyptians were no longer the invaders and conquerors. They were now the ones hemmed in by hostile forces. An understanding of who these forces were and where they originated will be critical to our understanding of the imperial collapse.

The largest casualties among the foreign groups accompanying the Libyans were suffered by the Akyawash, identified by early translators with the Achaeans. Achaean is a name we have associated with the Mycenaean Empire. Their losses were around 2,400 by count of severed hands and phalluses. If indeed the Mycenaean Empire, or city-state within the Empire, were deploying sizeable forces against the borders of Egypt proper, a second clash of empires was likely in the offing.

According to contemporary Egyptian records, Merneptah's forces carried the day when the Libyan king decided that discretion was the better part of valor and quit the field, demoralizing his followers. It is likely that the Egyptian forces prevailed because they retained a powerful chariot force and the associated mobile projectile delivery capability. The lack of capture of any enemy chariots by the Egyptians establishes that the entire Libyan force, allies included, was reliant on infantry.

Capture records of other items shed some light on the Libyan force. Listed are almost 130,000 arrows (more properly quivers and arrows), which suggests a large foot archery service. Over 9,000 swords speaks to a large infantry force. The actual numbers given are precise to the integer rather than being rounded off, which indicates they were extracts from actual field reports rather than simply inflated propaganda.

The Egyptian victory was tempered by the fact that the days of imperial expansion had passed. Their battles were now to simply hold what they had taken in generations gone by. For all the imperial struggles and setbacks the Egyptians encountered during this period, the 13th Century BC was kinder to them than it was to the Hittites.

THE HITTITES AFTER KADESH

U<small>NLIKE THE</small> E<small>GYPTIANS, THE</small> H<small>ITTITES</small> had neither the stable agricultural base provided by the Nile nor a ready source of gold such as Nubia. Their wealth, and by extension their ability to maintain a strong military, came from whatever the component states of their empire could provide in the way of taxes and levies. A significant portion of the wealth of component states had its foundation in international trade. This was a serviceable model for the Hittite Empire at the beginning of the 13th Century BC. Robust trade meant a steady revenue stream to maintain its military, which in turn could be used to secure the commercial centers and trade routes on which its wealth was based.

In the aftermath of Kadesh, however, the negative side of the situation arose. Sizeable battle losses had to be replaced. Trade is dependent on demand for goods. It cannot be expanded in response to political or military need. The economic situation is illustrated by a bit of contemporary writing from the Canaanite city of Ugarit, a Hittite vassal state at the time. In it the city's king agrees to waive the duty to report shipments arranged by a specific merchant family. In other words, no tax was due. Tax relief was being used to keep entrepreneurs loyal to the city, much as modern states offer incentives to attract industry. Any attempt to tinker with the tax system to increase imperial revenue could have just the opposite result if merchants could find a better deal elsewhere.

As important a component of the tax base as trade was, the largest taxable segments of Late Bronze Age economies were agriculture and animal husbandry. These cannot be expanded beyond the constraints of arable land. The Hittite Empire faced the daunting task of rebuilding the expeditionary army that had been crippled at Kadesh on a fixed income. To complicate matters, there was no leisure for rebuilding. The army was needed in the field on a full time basis to secure the imperial borders and enforce the spear-point diplomacy that held the Empire together.

Muwatallis II died two years following the stalemate at Kadesh, after installing his brother Hattusalis III as administrator in Syria. He left the throne to his son, Mursilis III. A power struggle ensued. Hattusilis III succeeded in exiling Mursilis III and emerged as Hittite King around 1266 BC. By this time the Hittites could entertain little hope of imperial expansion beyond their current borders. The Amurru region had been recaptured, as well as other minimal losses during the pre-Kadesh campaigns of Seti I and Ramses II. Despite some continued campaigning, the border situation had settled into an uneasy stalemate. The Hittites were facing more urgent challenges on the Eastern border of their Empire.

The kingdom of Mitanni had fallen under Hittite domination during the campaigns of Suppiluliumas I. The Hurrians of Mitanni were by the mid 13th Century BC closely integrated with the Hittites. They were expert charioteers, and at one point the chief of Hittite chariotry was a Hurrian. They served as vassals and as a buffer state between the Hittite Empire and the hostile Mesopotamian kingdom of Assyria.

The Assyrian kingdom began as a minor state centered at the city of Ashur, on the Upper Tigris River. For a time Assyria was ruled by the Kingdom of Mitanni, but managed to gain independence and grow in size and military power. The flash point between Mitanni and Assyria was a revolt in the province of Urautru, in the Southern part of modern Armenia. The Assyrian king, Shalmaneser I, mounted a retaliatory expedition. The Mitanni, with the help of the Hittite garrison, moved to block the Assyrian advance.

In 1263 BC the combined Mitanni-Hittite effort failed. The Assyrians broke the blockade and went on a destructive rampage through Mitanni. Shalmeneser I's claim that he devastated one hundred eighty Hurrian cities and destroyed the Hittite army may have contained elements of propaganda. The majority of the Hittite army was certainly deployed in regions beyond his reach. However, the Hittites did suffer a significant blow to both their military power and their economy.

The loss of a portion of the Hittite army and the resurgence of an Assyrian threat on their eastern border would have required re-deployment of Hittite forces away from the border with Egypt. The obvious option to securing the border by force of arms was to negotiate a settlement of hostilities and set conditions under which both empires were likely to prosper. Hattusilis III also had interests other than military action, including the re-building of the capitol Hattusas, reform of the constitution and copying the royal archive. It is to him we are indebted for the trove of documents unearthed at Hattusas, without which we would be blind to much of Hittite history. The Hittites under Hattusilis III and Egyptians under Ramses II, who also had priorities of his own, were able to strike a deal and signed a treaty in 1258 BC. This resulted in a stable border between Syria and Canaan and eliminated Egyptian motivation to support the Assyrians.

Hattusilis III's military issues included not only border security on the Empire's eastern flank, where the Assyrians were a threat, but also a revolt in Western Anatolia in the Aegean coastal region. A renegade named Piyamaradus had defeated a Hittite vassal king in the area and was attempting to carve out an independent kingdom, probably with help from the Mycenaeans. Part of a diplomatic letter written to the Ahhiyawan (Mycenaean) king survives in the Hittite archives. In the letter the Hittite King complains that Tawagalawa, the brother of the Mycenaean King, had forsaken an earlier close relationship with the Hittites and provided aid and sanctuary to Piyamaradus.

The earlier relationship between the Mycenaeans and Hittites is not specified, but since the letter refers to Tawagalawa mounting or riding the chariot of the Hittite King, it was probably military in nature and may have involved providing Mycenaean mercenaries to fight in the Hittite army. The letter also complains of an unspecified incident at Wilusa in northwest Anatolia. Scholars have speculated that the Hittite Wilusa and the Greek Troy (Ilios in the *Iliad*) are the same. This is debatable; however the *Iliad* does refer to an earlier sack of Troy by the Greek hero Herakles, which supports the notion of ongoing hostilities in the region. True or not, Hittite control within the Empire was eroding, and the Hittites, who were in a position to know, put at least part of the blame on Mycenaean designs on, and activity in, the area of northwest Anatolia.

Hattusilis III was succeeded by his son, Tudhalyis IV, in 1238 BC. Tudhalyis IV was defeated by the forces of the Assyrian King Tukulti-Ninurta at the Battle of Nihriya around 1237 BC. Little is known about the battle, but the outcome marked the beginning of a dramatic shift in the power structure in the Near East. A treaty between Tudhalyis IV and a ruler in the Amurru region specifies that no Ahhiyawan ship was to be allowed to reach the Assyrians, strongly suggesting Assyrian encroachment as far as the Eastern Mediterranean coast.

Tudhalyis IV, trapped between Mycenaean ambitions on the west and Assyrian ambitions on the east also had to deal with other issues. For reasons not made clear in contemporary writing but possibly due to the loss of access to copper-rich areas on the Empire's eastern frontier, Tudhalyis IV mounted an expedition to take over the island of Cyprus. Late Bronze Age battle artifacts such as bronze arrowheads and lead sling pellets have been found on Cyprus, supporting the notion of conflict at the time.

As a side note, it was Tudhalyis IV who had the pantheon of Hittite gods carved into stone near the Capitol of Hattusas. We can only wonder whether his problems had grown so numerous and daunting that he turned to divine intervention as a last hope. With Tudhalyis IV's death around 1207 BC, the story of the Hittite Empire grows murky. Less is known of the two succeeding kings, Arnuwandas III and Suppiluliumas II. Suppiluliumas II boasts in a contemporary tablet of re-conquering Cyprus after a naval battle. Tudhalyis IV's triumph must have been fleeting if the Cypriots were able to throw off the Hittite yoke and raise a fleet of ships.

Contemporary records contain accounts of emergency shipments of grain among Hittite vassal states during the late 13th Century BC. Some recent scientific evidence of drought exists but, had it been widespread, there would have been no grain to share. This may have been a situation such as occurred in modern times in the Horn of Africa, where food was available but the distribution system broke down. Vassal states that had flourished by specializing in areas other than agriculture would have been dependent on the Empire for food. Their privation was a signal that the Empire was tottering toward collapse.

When archaeologists found the city of Hattusas, it was, for a 3,000 year old ruin, remarkably intact. The passage of more than three millennia had taken its toll, but the city remained above ground and no settlement had been built on top of it, indicating that it had simply been abandoned. The water supply system would have been functional at the time of its abandonment. The palace area was burned but it is not possible to tell whether this was arson or accident. The passage of time could account for the condition of the walls, and has certainly obscured any evidence of hostile breach of the defenses. The artifacts of Late Bronze Age battle, in particular bronze arrow heads and lead sling pellets, are notable by their absence.

We have found written records for Hittite activity immediately prior to 1200 BC, but we have nothing describing the abandonment of the city. Given the meticulous state of Hittite record keeping, this suggests that the abandonment was not an organized event. It may not have been a single occurrence, but rather a succession of departures as the city, without immediate supporting agriculture, became progressively less tenable. In one contemporary document, Suppiluliumas II chides the vassal kingdom of Ugarit for falling behind in deliveries of grain needed in the capitol.

The decline of the Hittite Empire in the 13th Century BC began after a subtle shift in the imperial model. During the early and middle years of the Hittite New Kingdom, the royal archives supported by numerous contemporary sources show conquest bringing expansion which paid for investment in future conquest. By 1300 BC the Hittite Empire had reached its practical limits and was hemmed in by forces too powerful to permit future expansion. Egyptian aggression threatened the southern border. The Assyrians blocked the way east. The Mycenaeans held the Greek mainland and Islands to the west. The Kaska bedeviled the Hittites from the north.

The Hittite Empire was by then the keystone of a vast Eastern Mediterranean trade network. Trade took the place of expansion as the economic underpinning of the Empire. The Uluburun shipwreck in the context of the large fleets available at the time and numerous contemporary trade documents establishes that the trade was both massive and lucrative. As long as the Hittite military could secure the status quo, the Empire would remain viable.

The destruction of a large chariot force at Kadesh cost the Hittites a significant portion of their advantage in projectile delivery, the capability that allowed the few to dominate the many. The importance of Kadesh cannot be overstated. It was the first major direct clash of the Eastern Mediterranean Empires of the Late Bronze Age. It was recognized as pivotal at the time, in particular by the Egyptians who included its narrative in many monumental structures.

Losses at Kadesh, by themselves, did not cause the decline of the Empire. They simply began a process of de-stabilization. The Hittite economy and the time required for training limited the pace at which the chariot corps could be rebuilt. Additional reverses through the Mitanni alliance further degraded Hittite ability to maintain a robust military. The Assyrians did not just inflict significant damage on the Hittite army. They also destroyed a large number of Hurrian cities, and with them sources of revenue the Hittites might have used to rebuild their military.

The Hittites were able to mitigate the external threat to a limited extent by negotiating a peace treaty with the Egyptians. The Assyrian threat loomed large, and the constant threat from the Kaska tribes on the northern border remained. The Mycenaeans threatened inroads in Western Anatolia. Internal pressures mounted.

The Hittite Empire was a series of enforced alliances. The enforcing army consisted of a central core of Imperial troops buttressed by forces from vassal cities and by groups of mercenaries. With declining fortunes, the ability to pay and reward troops also declined. Mercenary units would have been cast adrift to fend for themselves. Lacking viable commercial skills, they would be tempted to plunder. The Hittite military force, reduced in size, would be progressively less able to defend against encroachment and raiding, and enforce the alliances that held the Empire together.

The result was a degenerative cycle in which the Hittite Empire, without resources from vassal entities was unable to maintain the imperial troops needed to hold the vassal entities in thrall. This eventually reverberated to the Imperial capitol. It is possible that Hattusas was sacked by disgruntled defenders, or the defenders may simply have left to pursue other opportunities in the cities of their origin. In any event, the Hittite imperial business model failed and the Empire essentially imploded.

Absent comprehensive contemporary records it is not possible to trace the Hittite Empire to a specific end point. What information we do have suggests that the Hittite kings soldiered on into the 12th Century BC, trying to salvage what they could of the realm. It was a hopeless task and eventually all that remained were pockets of the old culture, the largest of which seems to have been centered at the city of Carchemish.

The post-imperial cultures are referred to by modern scholars as Neo-Hittite. As a scatter of remnants it had no significant military or economic influence. Persian conquests as few centuries later marginalized it even further and the conquests of Alexander the Great obliterated the last remnants. While the later Neo-Hittite culture was without influence, the waning of the Hittite Empire around 1200 BC had a profound impact on the imperial equilibrium of the Eastern Mediterranean.

TRADE, TROY AND THE MYCENAEANS.

THE MYCENAEANS LEFT NO IMPERIAL archive. Their empire simply evaporated into the mists of time. It was once thought, based upon Greek historical writing from the 1st Millennium BC, that northern immigrants called Dorians displaced the Mycenaeans. This idea had to be discarded when archaeological evidence placed the rise of Dorian culture several centuries after the fall of Mycenaean civilization. We are left to infer the fate of the Mycenaeans based on archaeological findings, snippets of contemporary writing and later Greek literature.

Dramatic literature is not automatically invalid as historical source material. The fact that Margaret Mitchell's *Gone With The Wind* is florid romance does not mean that the American Civil War did not happen. On the contrary, literature is often most compelling when it has as its foundation major historical events. The Roman poet Virgil based his *Aeneid* on the legend that the city of Rome was founded by a fugitive Trojan prince named Aeneas. Archaeology has established that Rome dates from centuries after the Trojan War, and the legend had long been regarded as pure fable. Recent DNA analysis, however, established that markers from Rome's precursor Etruscan civilization in Italy could be traced to an area south of Troy. One value of literature in historical research is that it has often crystallized around a kernel of fact.

How much fact exists at the kernel of Homer's *Iliad* and *Odyssey* is open to question. The belief persists among scholars that Homer compiled a body of work developed over centuries by minstrels and handed down orally from one generation to the next. The notion of an oral tradition has a certain romantic allure, but it does not address the question of why the written versions were produced at all. Cultures with a tradition of maintaining oral histories tend not to write them down.

Writing allows outsiders to pry into their past and their beliefs. Greek poets also had considerable economic disincentive. A prime market for the written version was among the wealthy and educated. This was the segment of the population that could pay most lavishly for poetic recitations. In addition, rival groups could easily seize on the material and destroy any monopoly the guild of minstrels enjoyed.

It is possible that both Homer's works and other tales of adventure are not compilations of oral traditions but copies or abstracts of written works dating back to the Mycenaean period. In the centuries following the Mycenaean collapse, written language changed drastically. An easily mastered system of writing based on a few individual letters that could make up the full lexicon of spoken words replaced the previous combination of syllabic and symbolic writing that had been limited to a few Mycenaean scribes. If the *Iliad* and *Odyssey* existed in some form in Mycenaean Linear B, they would have to be converted to alphabetic writing to be used going forward. This does not do away with minstrels, who certainly existed, but rather raises the possibility that their work was based upon written material dating originally from the time of the Mycenaean collapse.

There has been some debate as to whether Homer's works accurately represent the Mycenaean period, based on their content. It is argued that Homer simply commingled fanciful tales of the Bronze Age Mycenaean Empire with the infantry war-fighting norms of the Iron Age. In fact Greek Iron Age infantry engagements looked nothing like the descriptions from the *Iliad*. They were clashes of poorly armored citizen soldiers equipped with only a thrusting spear. Archaeological evidence does exist to suggest that the epics of the Trojan War did come down in some direct fashion from Mycenaean history. Homer mentions a unique helmet made of boars' teeth worn by Odysseus. Such a helmet (although not necessarily the same one) has been found in Mycenaean context.

Homer's works were not the only dramatic pieces drawn from the history of the Trojan War. The *Iliad* and the *Odyssey* are two in a series of poems called the *Epic Cycle*. In chronological order of events, these begin with the *Cypria*, eleven books covering the time from the beginning of the war up to the *Iliad*. About fifty lines of this work survive. Following the *Iliad* are the *Aethiopis,* five books of which five lines survive, and the *Little Iliad,* four books of which about thirty lines survive. These cover the death of Achilles and the building of the Trojan Horse. The sack of Troy, called the *Iliou Persis,* and the return of the Achaeans to Greece, called the *Nostoi,* cover another seven books which also survive as fragments and bridge the gap to the *Odyssey.* The survival of fragments establishes that the works did exist, but the fact that they did not survive intact leaves us to rely on summary and reference.

We know the general content of the *Epic Cycle* from a summary contained in a work called the *Chrestomathy* of Proclus. This work also no longer exists, and no one knows for sure who Proclus was, but we do have a summary of Proclus' summary in the preface of the Venetus A manuscript of the *Iliad* prepared the in 10th Century AD. This summary itself is incomplete and is missing the *Cypria,* but we have some knowledge of that from another work called the *Bibliotheca* of Photius, possibly also an extract from the *Chrestomathy* of Proclus.

Beyond the fact that we are working from second and third generation reference, there is also the question of how much is history and how much is merely theater. The *Cypria* and *Little Iliad* were criticized by no less an authority than Aristotle for being poor poetry because they had too many story lines. This suggests that a literary veneer was laid over a complex framework of historical fact. Stripped of obvious theatrical elements, this framework can provide clues to the last days of the Mycenaeans.

Another literary work that offers insight into the closing chapter of the Mycenaean Empire is the *Voyage of Argo.* This is the familiar legend of Jason and the Argonauts venturing to the land of Colchis in search of the Golden Fleece. The work is crafted as theater, but has its foundations in verifiable fact. Archaeological evidence shows that Mycenaeans had at least established trade relations in many of the area where Jason ventured. The ancient land of Colchis is the Black Sea coast of the modern Republic of Georgia. Animal skins were used in the region as part of the process of extracting gold, which lends further credence to the idea that there may be a kernel of truth in the story.

The voyage continues beyond Colchis into Europe. The geography, including trips along several rivers and overland portages, is accurate. While this does not conclusively establish that the story was based on real events, it does suggest that it was not wholly imaginary. Modern replication of portions of the voyage establishes it in the realm of the possible.

The version of the *Voyage of Argo* that exists today dates from the Hellenistic period, the time following the conquests of Alexander the Great. During the Hellenistic period brevity was preferred in literary works. The author, Apollonius of Rhodes, apparently presented one or more longer versions, but was compelled to shorten the work for publication. The currently available version was abridged from a much longer original from earlier classical times. It appears to originate from the same source as the Homeric epics. Based on a reference to the son of Jason in the *Iliad*, the *Voyage of Argo* would have taken place a generation earlier.

The survival of heroic tales from Mycenaean times suggests that they related to a major cultural shift that left audiences longing for lost power and prosperity. A similar situation surrounded the crafting of the later Northern European epic *Beowulf.* Christian converts nostalgic for the good old pagan days compiled their cultural memories. *Beowulf* can be traced to the time of known king killed in a raid around 520 AD, We are not as fortunate with the Greek epics, but every indication is that they reflect, at least in background detail, the last days of the Mycenaeans.

From the *Iliad* we gain a sense of a feudal society bound together by strict codes clearly understood and obeyed by the participants. There is an overlord, Agamemnon with his scepter, but he can be challenged by Achilles when the division of the spoils of war is not conducted according to code. While the system of governance is portable, that is, it applies equally whether the participants are in their home territory or on a foreign battle field, the encampments; lines of authority and specific identities of the component states are strictly segregated and maintained. Each entity is distinct but all are subordinate to the Empire.

From the *Cypria* we learn that when neither Achilles nor Odysseus was keen on an expedition to Troy they had to resort to chicanery in an attempt to evade duty rather than to challenge the Imperial decision to undertake the expedition. Neither man succeeded and the Imperial will was done.

The *Odyssey* provides insight into the internal workings of the city-state of Ithaca, nominally ruled by Odysseus under the feudal code but to a large degree under the de-facto control of influential citizens when the king was away at war, or missing following the conflict. On his return Odysseus must regain his kingdom by force of arms.

The *Voyage or Argo* provides a different perspective. Here the focus is economic. A shipload of adventurers is sent generally northward to seek new riches. This suggests city-states, and by extension an empire, dependent on commerce for prosperity, if not outright survival. From literature we have a picture of an empire possessing built-in potential lines of fracture. The two main themes of the stories are war and commerce.

Fitting this picture into the context of the 13th Century BC, the sequence of the Mycenaean collapse begins to take shape. In the first quarter of the century, during the campaigns leading up to Kadesh, the Mycenaean Empire would have been admirably equipped to supply a thriving market for mercenaries. Each city-state had trained infantry with an existing command structure, and all were bound together by a common culture and language, facilitating control. During the same period Mycenaean city-states traded extensively in the Eastern Mediterranean, as evidenced by the presence of Mycenaean artifacts on the Uluburun shipwreck and by pictorial representations of large fleets of ships in earlier Minoan context.

Following Kadesh, the market for mercenary labor would have suffered due to reduced campaigning. On the plus side, the Hittite-Egyptian peace treaty would have secured the existing trade corridor from the Aegean Sea south to Nubia, with branches into the rich markets of Mesopotamia. This meant an unimpeded flow of raw materials and finished goods feeding the Eastern Mediterranean sea trade, as well as providing extensive markets for Mycenaean pottery, comestibles and other goods.

To a large extent Mycenaean prosperity depended on the continuing strength of the other two empires, and in particular that of the Hittites. As the Hittite Empire faltered in the face of Assyrian advances, the Mycenaeans sought direct trade with the Assyrians. The Hittites moved to block Mycenaean access to the Eastern Mediterranean coastal area where the Assyrians appear to have encroached. By 1225 BC there had appeared in at least one Hittite contemporary document an indication that the Hittite King no longer considered the Mycenaean King an equal. A contemporary shipwreck off the coast of the port city serving Mycenae was far smaller than the Uluburun wreck, suggesting seriously reduced commercial activity. The *Voyage of Argo,* possibly launched about the same time, represented an attempt, necessary if not desperate, to find new sources of commerce.

Not long after, Mycenaean military elements aligned with the Libyans for a thrust into Egypt. The Egyptian Pharaoh Merneptah drove them back with heavy losses in 1207 BC. Absent success elsewhere, the remaining target of opportunity was the failing Hittite Empire.

Following the abandonment of the Hittite capitol of Hattusas around 1200 BC, the Mycenaeans launched an expedition into Hittite territory around Troy. The dates of 1194 to 1184 BC assigned to the Trojan War by the later Greek historian Eratosthenes may be accurate. Revised dating by seriation and stratigraphy places the destruction of the city at level VIIa of Troy around 1180 BC. The scale reported by Homer, one thousand ships and fifty thousand men, rivaled the Hittite force at Kadesh, clearly more than would have been necessary to reduce a single city. The *Iliad* has the Achaeans clashing with numerous allies of the Trojans, probably former vassals of the Hittites, which they would have had to do in order to overrun the area.

Ultimately victory would have gained the Mycenaeans nothing beyond a little plunder. Previous Hittite trade routes feeding into northwest Anatolia had already broken down. This is not to suggest that trading came to an abrupt halt. Incentive still existed for entrepreneurs to risk the less secure land and sea routes, but movement of goods at the industrial levels needed to support the Mycenaean Empire was a thing of the past. With the neighboring imperial infrastructure that had secured their trade failing, they moved to secure their position with both military expedition and commercial venture. When neither avenue prospered, the Empire was in a precarious position. Individual city-states were ripe for internal revolt.

The most likely scenario is that sketched in Homer's *Odyssey,* wherein powerful elements within the Kingdom of Ithaca move to usurp power. The pattern in modern revolt is remarkably similar. A quick glance at three examples is illuminating. The English *Magna Carta,* often seen as a first step away from palace rule and toward democracy was in fact tax reform forced on King John by his nobles. America's *Declaration of Independence* was signed by men of commercial substance, not by any lesser citizens. Russia's Bolshevik revolution, often cited as a rising of the masses to overthrow the Tsar, was nothing of the sort. The Tsar was removed by an elite under the Kerensky administration. They were in turn overthrown when the German Secret Service, eager to remove Russia from World War I, brought in a minor Russian aristocrat who had taken the Nom-de-Guerre Lenin to bring about a Bolshevik revolt. The vanguard of this revolt was the radicalized Russian Navy, and it was secured by foreign (Latvian) infantry.

Revolts in the city-states of the Mycenaean Empire would not have occurred in a vacuum. There would have been considerable impact on the physical infrastructure. Numerous Mycenaean sites have been excavated, and it is fair to ask if the findings support the idea of an internally disintegrating empire.

The city of Mycenae itself lends some support to the concept. It was expanded around 1250 BC, about the time the Hittite-Egyptian peace treaty would have had the effect of releasing armed and idle mercenaries back to the city-states that dispatched them. Mycenae was heavily fortified at this time, including the building of the signature Lion Gate. Some threat must have existed to prompt this level of effort and investment.

Other cities, including the previously mentioned Pylos, were destroyed around the end of the 13ᵗʰ Century BC. Here we have to be careful. Some authorities divide destruction into two categories, invasion or revolt if military artifacts are found in the ruins and earthquake if no such artifacts are found, and in particular if there is structural damage to walls. This reasoning is based on the lack of explosive munitions in the Late Bronze Age military arsenal. It ignores the fact the ancient cities were ticking time bombs.

The culprit is what is known in the modern era as a dust explosion. The requirements for such an explosion are s combustible dust with a high surface to volume ratio dispersed in sufficient concentration in an oxygen rich environment and an ignition source. They are a significant risk in modern silos. The most destructive dust explosion in the US occurred in 1878 AD, destroying the largest flour mill in the country as well as five other mills and taking more than three dozen lives. The most common use today is in making action films. Anyone who has witnessed a Hollywood pyrotechnic display has probably seen a controlled dust explosion.

Ancient cities were vulnerable as a result of their social structure. The elite, to maintain power, kept a stranglehold on food supplies. This often meant the storage of large amounts of grain in confined spaces in the palace or temple areas. The primary source of interior lighting at the time was some form of open flame. Dust explosions in a confined space can cause violent destruction as a result of overpressure and shock waves. A release of intense heat can ignite surrounding areas. Studies of items burned during the destruction by fire at ancient sites indicate that a powerful accelerant was required to reach the requisite temperatures. Melted gold has been found at some sites. Gold melts at over 1800 degrees Fahrenheit. The culprit is thought to be olive oil, also kept in quantity in palace or temple areas.

The destruction in Mycenaean cities was often centered on the palace area, with other areas relatively untouched. Earthquakes are not so selective. When widespread destruction did occur, it was the result of fire. Given the extensive use of timber in Mycenaean construction, a major conflagration could develop rapidly regardless of whether the source was accidental or the result of a social skirmish.

Possible evidence of social upheaval exists on the Island of Crete. Numerous mountain settlements appear in the early 12th Century BC, suggesting the exile of portions of the population from coastal cities, another sign supporting the idea of squabbling elites prominent in later Greek drama.

Perhaps more importantly, a significant number of mainland cities were simply abandoned. Notable among these was Corinth. As mentioned previously, the Isthmus of Corinth was seen as strategically important by following civilizations. Abandonment by the Mycenaeans suggests that there was no longer a civilization large or cohesive enough to be concerned with strategic locations. Destroyed cities were also abandoned rather than being built over as was the common practice in ancient times. A viable feudal empire simply evaporated.

The feudal governance system would not have disintegrated with the loss of cities. It was portable and would have remained as a set of organized entities. Those entities would have shared a common culture, language and military structure. While no longer an empire, they would still be capable of coordinated action. How they were able to successfully invade the previously inviolate territory of the Hittite Empire is another question.

THE ADVANTAGE SHIFTS

EMPIRE IS, BY DEFINITION, ROOTED in the ability of the few to dominate the many. During the Eastern Mediterranean imperial period of the Late Bronze Age this ability rested on the projectile delivery capability of large chariot armies. An effective chariot force required technically sound vehicles, matched horses, skilled drivers drilled in tactical maneuver and archers able to shoot powerful composite bows accurately from a moving platform at speed over uneven ground. As a result these armies were tremendously expensive to raise, train and maintain.

Imperial chariot armies had to be put to productive use to justify their cost. Potential employment fell into two categories, security and expansion. If the army was used exclusively for internal security, the taxes on existing agriculture and commerce had to pay for its upkeep. Otherwise imperial expansion was necessary to make up the difference. As long as successful campaigns were waged, the spoils of one could be applied to pay for the next. Successful armies could absorb the experienced fighters of defeated foes and grow in proportion to their victories.

The stalemate at Kadesh did not fit this template. If contemporary Egyptian records are correct, the Hittite chariot force was reduced to remnants. Even allowing for exaggeration, the damage had to be substantial. On the Egyptian side, the Re Division was destroyed, presumably along with its chariot contingent. The Amun Division was scattered out of its encampment and two other divisions saw heavy action. Egyptian losses may not have matched the Hittites' but they were sufficiently crippling to compel the withdrawal of Ramses II's expedition. Stalemate denied both empires the returns in loot they needed for immediate replacement of their losses. Re-building would have been a slow process and a drain on the imperial economies.

The Hittites suffered further chariot losses as a result of the military debacle when the Assyrians overran the allied kingdom of Mitanni. This left the Hittites facing a second major force rebuilding effort in little more than a decade, with no income to offset the cost.

On the Egyptian side, Ramses II was committed to a costly building program. Even if his new chariot factory in Pi-Ramses was able to meet the design output of 250 chariots per week, he still faced the expense of a long training program for horses and crews, as well as a significant ongoing outlay to maintain the force. The only use he would have for a force comparable to his Kadesh expedition was another potentially disastrous major foray into Syria. The logical, and actual, adjustment for both empires was to reach a peace agreement. This reduced the need for massive chariot forces and eased the financial burden on the Egyptians and the Hittites.

Reducing the size of standing chariot armies also reduced the comparative advantage of the few over the many. Massed infantry was still a lucrative target for fast moving chariot archers. However, with fewer chariot forces available, aggressors might, supported by good intelligence, profit by attacking areas where no chariot forces could be deployed due to shortages.

The shift in advantage was a slow process. It is unlikely that massed infantry ever had any direct contact with opposing chariots. The risk to fragile vehicles, exposed horses and lightly armored crews would have been too great to justify charging into an infantry formation. Large foot armies would have the advantage only when no chariots opposed them. This became a possibility during the 13th Century BC. In the Years from 1274 BC to 1237 BC the Hittite Empire suffered major chariot losses to the Egyptians at Kadesh, reckoned to be the greatest chariot battle ever fought, and to the Assyrians at Mitanni and Nihriya. Each loss would have made it progressively more difficult for the Hittites to provide complete chariot coverage for the Empire.

One group certain to have noticed the change in composition of the Imperial Army was the mercenary contingent that served alongside the regular troops. As imperial resources dwindled, more and more mercenaries would find themselves unemployed. Mercenary commanders would be left with dissatisfied followers, mouths to feed and no source of revenue. The most obvious option was to divert the restless energy of their troops to exploit the Empire weakened by the lack of chariots and loot their former patrons.

The shift from mercenary to raider was not as simple as it may seem. Mercenaries were accustomed to fighting as part of a chariot based army. They would have lacked the structure for independent operations. Even without chariots, the imperial armies that would oppose them were far from helpless. Experienced imperial commanders had at their disposal disciplined contingents of infantry, foot archers and slingers. New tactical doctrine would have to be developed by the former mercenaries to overwhelm such forces. A revised suite of weapons would have to be adopted and mastered.

A visible shift in the armaments of infantry forces occurred in the 13th Century BC. Most noticeable is the rise of a style of sword known as Naue II. This is a short (blade length about two feet) bronze weapon both pointed and edged, so it could be used for both stabbing and slashing. Some modern scholars have seen this as an improvement over previous designs. When evaluated in the context of edged weapons employment, it in fact runs counter to both physical principles and contemporary practice.

Previously the only weapon designed for both stabbing and slashing was the dagger, used for close-range personal defense against unarmored assailants. It consisted of a hilt from which projected a pointed blade sharpened along both edges. The method of employment was to thrust the blade into an exposed vital area and withdraw it with a slashing motion intended to sever adjoining blood vessels and promote exsanguination. Warfare required more robust weapons. Normally these were purpose-built for either stabbing or slashing, but not both.

Stabbing was the province of the spear. The act of stabbing is essentially a ground-reaction movement employing Newton's Law that every action had an equal and opposite reaction. The feet are firmly planted and the large muscles of the core are energized in a coiling motion that is released through the hips, turning the shoulders and accelerating the spear forward with maximum force. The spear allows a two-hand hold to control this force and resist any counter-reaction when it contacts the target. The spear also allows a stand-off of several feet for the warrior wielding it, providing some protection from defensive reaction from the target.

The Naue II sword with its short blade and single-handed hilt offered neither of these advantages. The lack of stand-off protection would be a particular problem. Numerous Late Bronze Age pictorial representations show spear carriers with only weapons and no substantial armor or shields. The Naue II brought the need for shields, ranging from the small buckler type that is the staple of Hollywood sword and sandal epics to the full body type hung from the neck, as described by Homer in the *Iliad*. These appear in the shape of a figure eight in pictorial representations of the time, allowing the wearer to manipulate a sword at waist level in close quarters fighting. Needless to say, these were unwieldy. Alexander the Great, who had a later version of this sword some centuries in the future, preferred to fight with the lance. Even the warriors of the much later *Beowulf* are introduced as *spear-armed Danes.*

Prior to the development of the Naue II, swords of the Late Bronze Age, such as the Egyptian sickle sword, were purpose-built for slashing. They had curved blades, which concentrated the force used to wield them into a very small area of the edge, maximizing the number of pounds per square inch applied to the target. The Naue II sword had some blade curvature, but nothing like the blades of later sabers and scimitars which were primarily slashing swords.

The Naue II sword had only the advantage of flexibility. It allowed both modes of attack in a compact package. This would be advantageous only in a massed or close formation infantry assault, where fighting room would be at a premium, targets close at hand and opportunities to either stab or slash equally likely and probably fleeting. Other weapons would be needed until close combat was imminent. This seems to be the case in the *Iliad,* where heroes would sling swords over their backs and use spears as the initial method of engagement.

A second weapon becoming more common at this time was referred to as a javelin, although it looks nothing like the item thrown in modern field events. Surviving examples are more like elongated darts, three to five feet in length, with metal points. These were tapered from back to front, which would tend to stabilize them in flight, and may have been thrown with some sort of atlatl or other mechanical advantage. Some have been found marked with the names of owners, indicating that they were prized items to be retrieved from the field after a battle.

While thrown javelins are a form of projectile delivery, they lack the range, the velocity and the stability of a properly turned and fletched arrow launched from a composite bow. Their main advantage would be that they could be thrown one-handed by an advancing infantryman, allowing him to use his free arm to maneuver a shield against incoming missiles.

Infantry armies did have dedicated projectile delivery capability in the form of foot archers and slingers. Even with composite bows, however, they could not match the impact of chariot archers. Chariots could move quickly from their points of initial deployment and mass wherever they could best influence the battlefield action by delivering a decisive volume of arrows. A moving chariot offered a fleeting target. Foot archers could only remain static or travel with infantry, leaving them vulnerable. The foot archer was limited by the range of his weapon, while the chariot archer was limited only by the range of his vehicle.

The chariot had built empires, but its use diminished as the resources required to support its deployment grew scarce. This created an opportunity for forces that massed their destructive power as infantry rather than projectiles to prevail on the battlefield. Mercenaries hired to protect the imperial chariot armies would have seen the strength of those armies waning. When peace came, many found themselves unemployed. The natural tendency would be to turn to privateering. They didn't always succeed, but the tide was turning.

As 1200 BC approached, an era of massed infantry assault was at hand. The ability of the few to prevail over the many had waned. The consequences would be far-reaching.

THE SEA PEOPLE

T HE TERM SEA PEOPLE WAS coined by an Egyptologist in the Mid 19th Century AD. It appears nowhere in contemporary writing from the Late Bronze Age. Modern scholars use it as a convenience to describe a confederation of invaders who arose from unspecified origins toward the end of the 13th Century BC. They were first encountered by the Pharaoh Merneptah as part of the Libyan invasion of 1207 BC. Merneptah's inscriptions at Karnak identify the component peoples of the confederation as the Akyawash (possibly an Egyptian version of the Hittite Ahhiyawa), Sherden, Shekelesh, Teresh and Luca. Of these the Sherden were familiar, having served Ramses II as mercenaries at the battle of Kadesh.

Ramses III, who was the second Pharaoh to engage the Sea People, divided them into six groups. In addition to the Sherden there were the Weshesh, Peleset, Tjekker, Danuna and Shekelesh. Thirty years separated the two Pharaohs' engagements. The different groupings may indicate that the Sea People's confederation changed in composition over time. Alternatively, different elements may have participated in different actions.

The Danuna were identified by early translators as Achaean (Mycenaean), specifically as Homer's Danoi. The Peleset are generally identified as the Philistines, opponents of the Israelites in Judeo-Christian scripture. The identification is based on a contemporary Egyptian document known as the Harris Papyrus, which talks about the resettlement of the Peleset in Canaan. This is a key piece of evidence because it ties one element of the Sea People to a specific set of artifacts recovered by archaeologists. The remaining elements have spawned numerous origin and migration theories to explain their sudden appearance in the Eastern Mediterranean. None of these theories are well-supported or widely accepted.

Inscriptions commissioned by Ramses III at Medinet Habu had the Sea People making a conspiracy in their lands. Where the lands of the Sea People were is open to question. The original Egyptian word, shorn of extraneous vowels added by the process of transliteration, is *RWW*. *RWW* is thought to refer to either islands or coastal areas. This which would be logical for the Sea People, but offers no clue to geographic location.

Ramses III's scribes tell us that no land could stand before the invasion of the Sea People. Locations are cited by name, and include Khatte, Qode, Carchemish, Azwara and Alasiya. Most of these areas are known. Khatte was the Egyptian version of Hatti, the name given by the Hittites as a general reference to their homeland. By the beginning of the 12ᵗʰ Century BC, when the depredations of the Sea People were first recorded, the Hittite capitol had already been abandoned. Carchemish was a city-state that controlled a key crossing of the river Euphrates. Azwara was an area of Western Anatolia normally under Hittite domination. Alasiya refers to the Island of Cyprus.

Conspicuous by their absence are Tanaj and Keftu, the Egyptian names for the Greek mainland and the Island of Crete respectively. This suggests that the Sea People originated in what was by then the former Mycenaean Empire. A group migrating from the north or the west would have to either traverse or bypass the Mycenaean Empire to reach the Eastern Mediterranean. Bypassing meant a long sea voyage without resupply, rest or repair. Further complicating such a move is the fact that the Sea People, in spite of their name, had a large land contingent, including families and chattels. Moving this element from a coastal origin around the Mycenaean Empire would involve an arduous trek through Macedonia.

Archaeological evidence from the Island of Crete shows that some inhabitants moved from the fertile coastal plains and trading ports and established settlements on defensible positions in the inland mountains around 1200 BC. This is not a natural or logical migration, unless the migrating population was under some sort of threat. It has been proposed that invasion by the Sea People drove coastal dwellers into the mountains. This is a possibility, but it leaves questions unanswered. Among these are where the invaders originated and how they amassed the force required to overcome strongly defended city-states within the Mycenaean Empire. It also does not explain the absence of mention of Crete in the Egyptian summaries of the Sea People's depredations.

A more likely possibility is that the Sea People originated in the city-states of the Mycenaean Empire as a result of cultural or political schism among the population. In Late Bronze Age times, Homer's *Odyssey* tells us of the political and cultural turmoil when long absent warriors returned to find their places usurped by interests that remained behind. Odysseus had to kill his rivals to reclaim the Kingdom of Ithaca. Later works tell us that Odysseus himself was killed by his illegitimate son and that Agamemnon died at the hands of his wife and her lover, who were later killed by Agamemnon's son.

The combination of lore and timing suggests that the Sea People may have been elements left from the disintegration of the Mycenaean Empire. The idea of disintegration is supported by the fact that a good number of Mycenaean cities were simply abandoned. Disintegration rather than invasion might explain why the Egyptian records refer to the Sea People by individual names, possibly city-states of the former Mycenaean Empire. Uniformity of language, culture and military tactics would go a long way toward explaining how the Sea People were able to weld themselves into an effective invasion force.

The depredations of the Sea People read like something from the *Iliad.* A sea-borne invasion force arrives at the coast in transport vessels and ranges inland, looting and destroying, resorting to siege when necessary. There is no specific evidence that Egyptian record of incursion into western Anatolia by the Sea People represents an outsiders' view of the Trojan War, however the correspondence of time and place and the lack of evidence to the contrary raises the possibility. Dating the destruction of Troy to 1184 BC (following Eratosthenes), which is generally confirmed by seriation analysis of pottery, we can look to Greek lore to see what the Mycenaeans were up to in the following years. In the early part of the *Odyssey* King Menelaus of Sparta boasts of his activities following the fall of Troy, specifically that he went to the Egyptian lands and took treasure from foreign speaking people. This sounds like the Sea People's raids into Egyptian controlled Canaan.

Numerous cities along the coasts of what are now Syria, Lebanon and Israel were plundered and razed by the Sea People. Our detailed knowledge of events comes from a Canaanite coastal city called Ugarit. As with Pylos in Greece, Hattusas in Turkey and Amarna in Egypt, destruction or abandonment can preserve records that might otherwise be scattered or lost. Archaeological excavation has uncovered a trove of contemporary documents. Based on surviving records, the city appears to have put up stiff resistance and held out for some time. Contemporary writing says the city fell under siege. Mention of a solar eclipse allows accurate dating to a time not long after the fall of Troy. One letter identifies a people called the Sheleca (possibly the Egyptian Shekelesh) among the conquerors. The fact that Ugarit, long a wealthy and important vassal of the Hittite Empire, could not be relieved before it fell is clear evidence, if more were needed, that the Hittite Empire had lost dominion. This scenario was repeated all along the Eastern coast of the Mediterranean.

Direct contemporary documentation of the fall of a Canaanite city to invasion is important because it helps to eliminate other potential causes of imperial collapse. Among the suggested causes are earthquakes, rampant disease and climate change. These were not uncommon events in the Late Bronze Age and were handled as a matter of routine, although with varying degrees of difficulty. Had any of these factors been disproportionate in impact relative to historical precedent, the literate Egyptians and Hittites should have mentioned them prominently in their records.

The Sea People were not the sole, or even the primary cause of imperial collapse. Their ability to wreak havoc was based on the fact that the Hittite Empire had already been weakened to the point that it could not respond. This weakening probably led to the abandonment of many cities whose existence depended upon provisioning and taxing the many caravans involved in the region's once thriving trade. As trade withered, cities and even small kingdoms were no longer viable.

The best indication we have is that the incursions of the Sea People were spawned by the disintegration of the Mycenaean Empire. If this were not the case, then we are confronted with the highly unlikely scenario that tens of thousands of Mycenaeans vanished into thin air at the same time tens of thousands of Sea People materialized out of nowhere. Mycenaean disintegration and the collapse of the Hittites left only one Empire standing. The Sea People were moving inexorably toward Egypt, some by sea and others by land, with their households and worldly goods, ready to conquer and settle.

According to the Medinet Habu inscriptions, the Sea People made camp in the Amurru region, formerly the contested border between the Hittite and Egyptian Empires, and laid waste to everything around. Egypt was clearly next on their agenda. The Pharaoh, Ramses III, had a robust espionage network. He had ample warning not only of the Sea People's coming, but also of the details of their transport and tactical approach.

The Sea People displayed two salient weaknesses. First, their boats were used only for transport and were not equipped for fighting. Second, their land contingent did not have a chariot component and would have to fight as infantry. A further complication for the sea-borne portion of the force was lack of the composite bow, which delaminated on sea voyages. This limited archery capability. Ramses III would turn these shortcomings to his advantage.

The Sea People had encountered little trouble reducing individual cities with limited defenses. They had overwhelming numbers of infantry at their disposal and could, if siege became necessary, cut off a city by devastating the supporting agricultural lands around it and by cutting trade routes that brought in essential goods. Against this threat Ramses III had the advantages of a mobile professional army experienced in defending a unified nation, as well as significant chariot forces. He also had a riverine navy that could move effectively in the Nile Delta and along the coast. When the Sea People moved against Egypt in 1178 BC, he was ready with a two pronged defensive strategy.

The first component of Ramses III's defense was the use of ships to intercept the Sea People's transport vessels. Ramses III's ships were fitted for combat; the Sea People's were not. The fighting appears from contemporary visual representations to have involved archery and boarding. Ships of the Late Bronze Age were normally built from the shell inward, rather than by laying a keel and constructing framework on which the shell was fastened. This meant that they were not likely to have the heavy keels necessary for ramming. This is probable, but not certain. Rams recovered during archaeological exploration of a naval battle site from the later Roman Punic Wars showed that rams were trident-like metal projections that rode at or just below the waterline to pierce the hulls of opposing vessels. These would not necessarily have been visible in the Egyptian pictorial representations.

Visual portrayals and text from Medinet Habu indicate that Ramses III either lured the Sea People into an ambush or managed to intercept them as they were about to land. Egyptian archers are shown firing from both shore and from boats fitted with forward fighting castles. Since the Egyptians had only short intercept distances to sail from shore, their composite bows did not suffer the delamination caused by prolonged sea exposure. The Sea People arriving by ship were trapped and soundly defeated.

The second and decisive component of Ramses III's strategy involved the use of combined chariot and infantry forces against the Sea People approaching by land from Canaan. Little is reported about the actual fighting. The exact location of the battle is not known, however Ramses III was well prepared. Reports from the period leading up to the invasion show the purchase of numerous chariot horses and the acquisition of other arms. If the battle ran true to Late Bronze Age form, chariot borne archers provided a mobile projectile delivery capability that significantly out-ranged the Sea People's. Follow-up with superior infantry forces settled the matter.

Ramses III broke the defeated Sea People into their ethnic groups for resettlement in various areas. Some were settled in Egypt, where Ramses III made a point of declaring that they would be added to the tax rolls. At least one group, the Peleset, or Philistines, were settled in Canaan. Ramses III may have wished to form a buffer state against depredations by barbaric nomads. It is also possible that the Philistines already had a foothold in Canaan, and that settling them was less trouble than moving them elsewhere.

Ramses III managed to save Egypt as a nation, but as an imperial power its days were effectively over. Reports of shortages of goods suggest that the price of defense had begun to take its toll on the survivability of the regime. Schisms appeared and succeeding Pharaohs were not able to prevent a general drift toward separation of power between the Pharaoh and the increasingly aggressive priestly cults. The country moved into a period of friction between Upper and Lower Egypt.

The rise and defeat of the Sea People marked the twilight of the Eastern Mediterranean Empires. The Mycenaean Empire had fractured. Some of its cities would live on and grow to greatness later in the history of Greece, but the Empire was no more. Hittite culture remained in enclaves that would limp on until extinction. The Egyptians would withdraw from Canaan and maintain only Nubia as their empire. The nation survived but the Empire had eroded.

While we have gained significant insight from the writing and lore of the Empires, there remains another source from the Late Bronze Age to be examined.

The Bible Tells Me So

A s the Late Bronze Age empires of the Eastern Mediterranean disintegrated, contemporary writing grew sporadic. The Egyptians left an illustrated narrative of events within their sphere, but they were only spectators at the collapse of the Mycenaean and Hittite Empires. Contemporary tablets from Pylos and Ugarit give only slices of daily life in city-states. To build a comprehensive narrative, we will need to look at later writings and corroborate what we can with contemporary artifacts.

The best known later writing concerning the period, even accounting for the Homeric epics, is Judeo-Christian scripture. The Bible, as it has come down to us, is one of the most studied works in the world. This allows us to refer to its contents with some confidence that we at least know what we are reading, even if the contents cannot be taken as literal truth. Analysis of the Bible, sometimes called criticism, although not in a derogatory way, is divided into numerous categories. Not all of these analyses are of interest to us, but several are useful.

First is textual analysis, which attempts to determine the most reliable text. Over time, unintentional errors creep into any work. One famous example from *Exodus* is the parting of the Red Sea. It turned out that this was a mistranslation. The original Aramaic reference was to the *Sea of Reeds*, a marshy area in the Nile delta which is passable on a seasonal basis. This is more believable, if less dramatic. Some intentional deviations are also possible. Many ancient sects with special interests made slight modifications to text, and textual analysis attempts to ensure that these have been weeded out by examination of different older manuscripts.

The second criticism of interest is form analysis. This is based in the belief that the Bible was brought together from older oral or written lore.

This includes genealogies, which can assist with dating, and narratives about ancient heroes, which can provide clues and corroboration.

The third is historical criticism. This is an analysis based on historical methods from other fields that tries to determine who wrote various segments of text, when they were written and in what setting. The text often reveals much about the society in which it was written. Interestingly, some of the tablets excavated from Ugarit contain stories parallel to those in the Bible, suggesting Canaanite origin. In this analysis, we can also include redaction criticism, which speaks to the society in which final editing occurred.

The Old Testament is thought to have been compiled in the last decades before 500 BC. This was a time of turmoil in Canaan. Around 600 BC the area known as Judea had been conquered by the Babylonians. In the Biblical version of events a large segment of the population was taken in slavery to Babylon. Recently discovered contemporary tablets written by members of the Judean population of Babylon suggest they went voluntarily in pursuit of commercial and administrative opportunities. The Babylonian Empire was defeated in 539 BC by Darius of Persia, who returned the expatriates (or more properly their descendants) to Canaan. Darius may have wanted to create a buffer state between his empire and Egypt, or he may simply have wanted to purge the existing administrative and commercial network of any residual alliance to the former overlords. Whatever his motivation was, a sizeable repatriation occurred.

Repatriation raised two difficulties for the priests of Judaism. First, their followers would call a basic tenet of priestly teaching into question. Specifically, if God gave them the Promised Land, why did he allow many of them to be carried out into slavery as the priests claimed? Second, there was considerable friction between those returned from Babylon and those who had never left over who would control Judea. The priesthood needed a unified message that would help bring their followers into line.

The message, as with any religion, was the omnipotence of the deity. The method seized upon was to collect all the available historical scrolls, plus any available oral tradition and lore, and recast their contents as a display of the power of God. In some cases two versions of the same story, for example the Flood, were included. This would allow the priests who read scripture to the illiterate to tailor their presentation to the beliefs of a specific sect. Also inserted were numerous anecdotes emphasizing the wisdom and authority of elders and clan leaders, since a patriarchal society requires the obedience of the populace to function.

The advantage to us is that to be effective, even though the message might be slanted, the text had to be true to accepted lore and written history. Since the compilers of the Old Testament were not specifically interested in recording and dating the precise events of history, it is left to us to sort out the relevant passages.

The two books most often thought of as reflecting the Late Bronze Age are *Joshua* and *Judges*. *Joshua* is the source of the theory of the external conquest of Canaan by the Hebrews who fled Egypt during the Exodus. *Judges* is the chronicle of a sequence of rulers who followed the conquest but were not sufficiently powerful to assume kingship.

In order to fit the two Biblical books into the context of Late Bronze Age imperial collapse, we need to establish dates for the contents of the books. The narrative of *Joshua* concerns the conquest of Canaan by the Hebrews when they emerged from their wandering in the desert following the Biblical Exodus from Egypt. The core story is that Hebrews were held as slaves in Egypt until one of their number, Moses, challenged an un-named Pharaoh to release them. God, the readers are told, hardened the Pharaoh's heart and he refused, whereupon God sent down ten plagues to demonstrate his power and permitted the Hebrews to escape.

The Bible (I Kings 6:1) specifically dates the exodus at 480 years before Solomon built his temple, which equates to around 1450 BC. This is all but impossible, since it would have occurred during the reign of the warrior Pharaoh Thutmoses III when Canaan, the ultimate destination of the Hebrews, was heavily garrisoned by Egyptian troops.

One modern theory attributes the ten plagues of *Exodus* to the volcanic winter and subsequent seismic events associated with massive Santorini eruption of 1550 BC. This is used to argue for the long standing thesis that the Exodus was a losers' eye view of the Hyksos expulsion, dramatized for religious impact. To date no confirming Egyptian documents have surfaced to raise this above the level of speculation.

A sizeable number of modern scholars prefer to date the exodus to the reign of Pharaoh Ramses II. This conclusion is based on two scraps of information. First is the mention in the Bible that the Hebrew slaves worked on the construction of the city of Pi-Ramses. This is not corroborated by any known Egyptian record. Second is a study of pottery distribution that indicates a rise in population in central Canaan around 1250 BC. This does not necessarily support in-migration. The Egyptian-Hittite peace treaty of 1258 BC would have led to substantial reduction in military levies of young males and led to an increase in the birth rate.

Absent a supportable date for the exodus, scholars turned to content to date the book of *Joshua*. Joshua's conquest of Canaan included the destruction of a catalog of cities. Archaeologists have spent decades excavating them. One aim was to scientifically date their destruction. The results produced dates spanning centuries. The summary conclusion is not necessarily that *Joshua* does not contain some kernel of fact, but rather that its vague timing and lack of independent support renders it useless for our examination.

The stories in *Judges* are more firmly fixed in the time of imperial collapse. Scholars generally ascribe a beginning date of 1200 BC, shortly after Pharaoh Merneptah's foray into Canaan, and an end date of 1020 BC for the events of *Judges*. From Egyptian records, specifically the Harris Papyrus, we know the Peleset were resettled in Canaan by Ramses III after the 1178 BC defeat of the Sea People. These have been identified as the Biblical Philistines. The last of the Judges, Samson, was a particular foe of the Philistines. From biblical text we know the names of the five primary Philistine cities, Gaza, Ashkelon, Ashdod, Ekron and Gath.

Archaeological work at Ekron has particular significance for our examination. In that city was found a building in the style of a Mycenaean megaron. In addition, Philistine pottery, locally made, was in the style of Mycenaean Late Helladic IIIc. This style was going out of fashion in the early 12ᵗʰ Century BC. Combined with a lower quality of manufacture, this suggests a culture spawned in the Mycenaean Empire, replicating the products of that culture as best they could. Loom weights of Mycenaean style were also found during excavations at the city. In short, at least one element of the Sea People was definitely Mycenaean in origin.

Archaeological excavation on the island of Cyprus has turned up similar artifacts from the time following the Sea People's invasion. There have been suggestions that Mycenaeans arrived on Cyprus in the wake of the Sea People. This is highly unlikely. There was no reason for the Mycenaeans to relocate their culture to an island off the coast of Anatolia unless they arrived as invaders.

A specific group of Sea People, the Tjekker, are associated with the coastal city of Dor, near modern Haifa. This association is established by a 12ᵗʰ Century BC papyrus known alternatively as *The Report of Wenamun* or *The Misadventures of Wenamun,* according to whether it is thought to be the journal of an actual voyage or an amusing work of fiction. In either case, the Tjekker would have had to have been known to occupy Dor for the audience to accept the work. Excavation at Dor is ongoing and may shed some light on the specific origin of the Tjekker.

While the Old Testament book of *Judges* is a compilation of lore peripheral to the collapse of the Eastern Mediterranean empires, it does help establish the Sea People as Mycenaean in origin. This conclusion dovetails with the timing of the disintegration of the Mycenaean Empire, established by archaeological findings, and Egyptian reports of the movements of the Sea People.

Homer's tale of the assault on Troy and related tales of its destruction in the *Epic Cycle* may well have been the Greek version of Ramses III's invasion of the Sea People into Anatolia. The tactics at least are similar; isolating a city by laying waste to the lands around it and then reducing its defenses by whatever means were at hand.

Prominently mentioned in Homer's *Odyssey* is the boast of King Menelaus of Sparta that he went to the Egyptian lands and took treasure from foreign speaking people. This closely matches events in Canaan associated with the depredations of the Sea People. It is not something a poet would randomly invent five hundred years later. It can only be lore from one of the city-states that survived the disintegration of the Mycenaean Empire.

Based on reported events and lore it is possible to construct a narrative of the group later christened the Sea People. Around 1225 BC the Mycenaean Empire disintegrated, with some of its component city-states surviving as individual entities. In 1207 BC some of these city-states allied with Libya in a failed invasion of the Nile Delta and were repulsed with heavy losses by Pharaoh Merneptah. Thereafter, according to the records of Ramses III, they entered into a conspiracy in their lands. This resulted in a large scale invasion of Anatolia in 1194 BC, known in modern times as the Trojan War.

After the fall of Troy in 1184 BC, portions of the expeditionary force continued south. Using similar siege tactics, they reduced important cities like Ugarit and Kadesh. Some, though probably not all, of the leaders saw Egypt as their ultimate objective. The dissenters were content to take their loot and return home. The more ambitious were defeated in land and sea battles by Ramses III and resettled. Of those resettled, the Peleset or Philistines are established as Mycenaean by physical evidence in the form of artifacts recovered from their known cities.

Scholars have proposed multiple sources for the Sea People, but none of the theories address the central question of how a makeshift force was able to overcome organized and sometimes stoutly defended city-states along the route to Egypt. The Mycenaean Empire, while composed of city-states itself, was a cohesive fighting force employing a uniform tactical doctrine. The doctrine would have survived the disintegration of the Empire. In addition, member states had probably supplied mercenaries to cities in the Eastern Mediterranean and were thus familiar with the defensive schemes of those cities. There is no need to invent, nor any justification for inventing, migrations to explain the Sea People. The Mycenaeans and only the Mycenaeans both fit the necessary profile and are supported by archaeological evidence.

The question of why the Egyptians settled the Philistines in Canaan remains a matter of speculation. The presence of the Philistines and the Israelites did check the expansion of the Phoenicians, who are thought to be responsible for the destruction of the Tjekker city of Dor. What is known is that the Egyptians abandoned Canaan shortly thereafter, around 1150 BC. Clues as to why may lie in yet another source. Research in dendrochronology has revealed that tree rings worldwide were thinner in the years 1159 BC to 1142 BC. This indicates a lower level of water and raises the possibility of leaner crops.

This idea is supported by Egyptian documentation from the time, which speaks of shortages and inflation. Dissatisfaction was common. Ramses III was assassinated in 1155 BC as part of a coup attempt engineered within his own harem. His successors lacked his administrative skill, and things gradually worsened in Egypt.

Identification of the Sea People as remnants of the Mycenaean Empire clears up much of the confusion that has attached itself to the last days of the Eastern Mediterranean imperial period. We are now in a position to develop a narrative and timeline describing the imperial collapse.

THE CHAIN OF EVENTS

THE SIMULTANEOUS COLLAPSE OF THE three Eastern Mediterranean empires of the Late Bronze Age turns out, on closer examination, to result from a sequence of related events. The events and their sequence are rooted both in the general nature of empire and in the structures of the individual empires. By definition an empire is a group of states ruled over by a single authority. Methods of gathering the member states and exercising authority can vary widely. Each of the three Eastern Mediterranean empires had its own unique approach.

The Egyptian Empire was based on the concept of a core nation with absolute authority over contiguous satellite states. The dictates of the Pharaoh were enforced by a powerful army composed of an elite chariot corps supported by a mixed infantry of native Egyptians, captured conscripts and foreign mercenaries. Sons of the rulers of subjugated realms were brought to Egypt and immersed in Egyptian culture before being returned to their native lands to act as surrogate rulers.

The foundation of the Hittite Empire was spear-point diplomacy enforced by a chariot based army similar to that of Egypt. The Empire was centrally administered through a robust flow of communication, a sizeable body of which remains for us to examine today. Unlike the Egyptian model, the Hittite Empire was not based on a core nation that would be defended to the last drop of Hittite blood. The capitol of Hattusas was abandoned when circumstances dictated.

The Mycenaean Empire appears to have been a feudal system of city-states. Trade was key to its economy. Mycenaean goods have been found at great distances from their native Greece. The Empire's military capability existed on the city-state level; a fairly small chariot corps with a primary focus on infantry. Mercenary infantry was supplied to both the Egyptian and Hittite Empires. Based on lore dating from after the fracture of the Empire, the king of the pre-eminent city-state was accepted under the rules of the Mycenaean feudal system as the premier authority figure.

Uneasy co-existence left the three empires in de-facto control of the eastern rim of the Mediterranean. Based on the contents of the Uluburun shipwreck and information regarding fleet size, the Eastern Mediterranean was the major trade corridor of the time. The trade moved industrial quantities of everything from copper and tin, the foundational elements of the Bronze Age, to comestibles to decorative art to exotics from far off lands. It was fed by in large part by land routes from Mesopotamia, Europe and Africa. Vassal states of the centrally located Hittite Empire prospered servicing ships and caravans. Cities in all three empires grew rich specializing in producing for export, confident that their profits would allow them to import the food they needed and the luxuries they desired. By 1300 BC the Eastern Mediterranean trade had made the empires interdependent. If one were de-stabilized, the repercussions would be felt by all.

The centuries of expansion that gave the empires control of the Eastern Mediterranean were key to the imperial business model. The essence of empire is domination of the many by the few. The Egyptians and Hittites achieved this with the mobile projectile delivery capability of chariot archery. Chariot armies were expensive to build and maintain. The investment was repaid by the spoils of conquest, which encouraged continued expansion. Mutual borders meant that one empire's expansion could come only at the expense of another. By 1300 BC Egyptian expeditions were nibbling at the southern Hittite boundaries. Hittite reaction was inevitable.

The Battle of Kadesh in 1274 BC was the first time the Egyptian and Hittite Empires met in large scale confrontation on relatively equal terms. Egyptian Pharaoh Ramses II mounted a massive expedition to expand on the conquests made at Hittite expense by him and his father, Seti I. Hittite King Muwatallis had an even larger force in the field to reverse recent Egyptian gains. The result was a stalemate with neither empire realizing any return on their investment in military capital.

Battle losses on both sides were significant, particularly to the chariot corps. Chariot forces took years to build and train. The costs were proportionally high. With no proceeds of conquest and no possibility of expanding taxable commerce or agriculture, rebuilding proceeded slowly. In the years following Kadesh, clashes between the Hittites and Egyptians were reduced to limited border adjustment campaigns.

Both empires were fighting on multiple fronts. Ramses II campaigned in Nubia to the South. The Libyan threat from the west compelled him to built and garrison outposts beyond the limit of settlement in the Nile Delta. The Hittites faced constant harassment from the Kaska to the north. The spear point diplomacy that held the Hittite Empire together required frequent internal campaigns to suppress organized resistance. Pirates plagued both the Anatolian and Canaanite coasts, which formed the western boundary of the Hittite Empire. In the east their vassal kingdom of Mitanni was under threat from the Mesopotamian kingdom of Assyria, requiring the maintenance of a considerable garrison. The military forces of both Empires were stretched thin.

This had major consequences for the Hittite Empire. In 1263 BC, the Assyrians launched an assault against Mitanni. The Mitanni forces, including the Hittite garrison were overwhelmed, further degrading Hittite force and capability. The Hittite Empire lacked the military wherewithal to respond to border threats and at the same time maintain internal imperial integrity. The Egyptians lacked the military resources to exploit the situation, or perhaps were not willing to risk what they did have. In 1258 BC the Hittite and Egyptian Empires came to an accommodation and a peace treaty was signed.

The treaty produced an unprecedented era of peace that would have a profound impact on the Mycenaean Empire. Cessation of border campaigning by the Egyptian and Hittite armies had a disproportionate impact on the mercenary contingent. Since they were used to augment native troops, captured conscripts and vassal infantry, they would be the first dismissed during any reduction in force. The Mycenaean economic model was based in part on a strong demand for the fighting men of their city-states as mercenaries.

The other key component of the Mycenaean economy was the Eastern Mediterranean trade that supported all three empires. The conditions that brought about the treaty de-stabilized the trade network on which the Mycenaeans depended. The Hittite Empire was further weakened by a significant defeat inflicted by the Assyrians at Nihriya. Assyrian inroads didn't just impact the Hittites. The loss of stable Hittites trade routes reduced the steady supply of both raw materials to make Mycenaean products and imported foods to sustain the Empire, as well as reducing their income from export goods. Mycenaean efforts to establish direct trade with the Assyrians who had reached the Eastern Mediterranean coast were opposed by the Hittites.

Attempts to establish trade with the Assyrians date to 1234 BC. Exploration of trade opportunities in Europe, as chronicled in the later epic poem *Voyage of Argo,* probably date to a decade later. A shipwreck in Mycenaean waters dated to around 1200 BC and much smaller than the Uluburun wreck suggests the Eastern Mediterranean maritime trade had fallen off dramatically. The Mycenaean king had long since been marginalized in diplomatic correspondence.

Mycenaean city-states, perhaps acting independently of the Empire as the rules of confederation apparently permitted them to do, turned their attention to Egypt, and to an alliance, either on a mercenary or political basis, with the King of Libya, who was planning to invade and occupy the western portion of the Nile Delta. This resulted in their participation in the disastrous invasion of 1207 BC. Pharaoh Merneptah still maintained sufficient chariot forces for border defense. Chariot archery was still the decisive factor in land battles. Neither the Libyans nor the Mycenaeans were able to mount corresponding projectile delivery capability.

Backing losing efforts was not a productive use of the Mycenaean's sizeable infantry resources. More promising opportunities presented themselves to the Mycenaeans as a unified group. The ability of the Hittite Empire to control and maintain order in Anatolia, which lay at the geographic center of trade through the area, was waning. In 1194 BC the Mycenaeans, acting as a confederation rather than as an empire, invaded western Anatolia. Unlike the alliance with Libya, this was a

Mycenaean enterprise to expand the Mycenaean sphere of influence. The resulting ten year conflict has come down to us in lore as the Trojan War. When it ended in 1184 BC all that had been accomplished was the sack of Troy and surrounding cities.

With no market for its mercenaries and no trade to support the specialized production of member city-states, the imperial structure was no longer viable. Many of its component cities were by then either abandoned or destroyed. Feudal lords moved with their forces, families and worldly goods in a conquest of Canaan.

The Hittites found themselves gradually overwhelmed by a combination of military defeats and mounting internal problems. In the years before 1200 BC the Hittite capitol of Hattusas had been abandoned for the final time. The Empire probably continued into the 12th Century BC, although documentation is sparse and the details unclear. It is clear that by 1180 BC the Empire was no longer able to mount an effective defense of its vassal city-states. Many of those not already abandoned due to declining trade fell victim to opportunistic Mycenaean raiders.

The economy of Canaan was trade based, and was not self-sufficient. The Mycenaeans, now called by modern scholars the Sea People, were little better off for their conquests. The Sea People raided and plundered down the Eastern Mediterranean through the remains of the Hittite Empire, moving toward the riches of Egypt and the fertile Nile valley.

Egypt had a national identity and its economy, fed by the Nile and by Nubian gold, was still strong enough to mount a stout border defense. Infantry was the Sea People's primary asset. Pharaoh Ramses III had both chariot and naval capability. He decisively defeated the Sea People in 1178 BC and resettled them in Egypt and other locations where they could no longer regroup and pose a threat, but rather bolster the tax base and provide a buffer against hostile incursion.

Ramses III's successful defense of the homeland was costly and came at a time when Egypt's tax base was dwindling. The nation began to destabilize. Ramses III was assassinated in 1155 BC. Compounding matters, beginning in 1159 BC and continuing through 1142 BC, the climate dried measurably and shortages of basic goods became problematic. The Egyptians abandoned Canaan around 1150 BC and maintained only their holdings in Nubia.

The disintegration of the Eastern Mediterranean Empires was complete. The Hittites had fragmented into whatever minor centers of influence and culture remained after the devastation by marauding remnants of the Mycenaean confederation. Following the defeat of the Sea People by the Egyptians, the Mycenaean Empire was reduced to a few cities in Greece and scattered settlements maintaining the culture. The stage was set for what would follow.

Timeline of Imperial Collapse

Date	Mycenaeans	Egyptians	Hittites
1274 BC		**Battle of Kadesh** Stalemate crippled Egyptian and Hittite Armies	
1263 BC			**Assyrians Take Mitanni** Loss of Hittite Garrison
1258 BC	Loss of mercenary market	**Egyptian-Hittite Peace Treaty** Reduced Military strength	
1250 BC	**Mycenae Fortified** (Internal revolt?)		
1237 BC			**Assyrians Defeat Hittites** Assyrian encroachment
1234 BC	**Assyrian Trade Blocked** Economy crippled		
1225 BC	**Fracture of Empire** King no longer recognized		
1208 BC		**Revolt in Asiatic Empire** Put down by Merneptah	
1207 BC	**Libyan-Mycenaen Invasion of Nile Delta** Repulsed with heavy losses by Merneptah		
1200 BC			**Hattusas Abandoned** End of Hittite Empire
1194 BC	**Invasion of Anatolia** (Confederation of Cities)		
1184 BC	**Invasion of Syria and Canaan** (Sea People)		
1178 BC	**Failed Mycenaean Invasion of Egypt** Mycenaeans dispersed by Ramses III		
1150 BC		**Canaan Abandoned**	

AFTER THE APOCALYPSE

— ∾ —

It is an axiom of modern hubris that we should learn from the mistakes of history, lest we doom ourselves to repeat them. Those who preceded us were not fools, nor were they prone to mistakes. They pursued ambitious goals and assumed correspondingly large risks. The consequences of those risks may have destroyed what they built, but the process of building advanced the state of human knowledge and laid the foundation for further advancement.

The Eastern Mediterranean Empires of the Late Bronze Age were achievements of consolidation on a scale never before attempted. Interaction and geography made them the centerpiece of a trade system that reached west to the British Isles and east to Asia, south to Sub-Saharan Africa and north into Europe. Raw materials from distant sources became widely available in industrial quantities. Specialized manufacture became commonplace. New ideas and best practices followed the trade routes along with the material products of the makers.

The period following the imperial collapse is often referred to as a dark age. Some scholars have gone as far as to suggest that people forgot how to write. This is clearly not the case. Egyptian hieroglyphic writing persisted until the 4th Century AD, when it was wiped out in a wave of Christianization. Cuneiform did not die out until around 100 AD. In fact a revolution in writing was underway during this period.

The alphabetic style of writing in which this book is presented began in the Eastern Mediterranean as something called Proto-Canaanite. The use of symbols to represent individual letters originated around 1300 BC. It was the product of traders who needed a way to account for their business and engage in contracts more efficiently than the Akkadian cuneiform that was the outgrowth of an earlier failed empire would allow.

The Ugaritic writing that gave us insight into the last days of the city was in alphabetic form, using either 22 or 28 easily learned and remembered characters to form a near-infinite variety of words. Professional scribes who took years to master complex pictorial or cuneiform writing were no longer required. Anyone with motivation and minimal teaching could become literate. The concept survived the imperial collapse and flourished in the post-apocalyptic period when extensive formal training was often not available.

Our word alphabet comes from the first two Greek letters, alpha and beta. Greek pottery of the post-apocalyptic period had alphabetic script in the decoration. This means that humble potters knew how to write. There would be little reason for them to do so unless their clientele could read their messages. As literacy became more widespread, knowledge and new ideas moved more easily and rapidly.

The individual empires each left unique contributions to the modern world. The most familiar legacy of the Hittite Empire is iron. During the Bronze Age the primary use of iron, aside from decoration, was in the making of stout tools like plowshares and axes, where a mass of metal could withstand the shock of impact. The physical properties of iron make it inferior to bronze for some key purposes, such as making weapons. It does not hold an edge as well as bronze, and tends to bend under stress. There are stories of Vikings having to pause in the midst of battle to straighten their iron swords.

The advantage of iron in ancient times was that it is a natural element, not an alloy. Ore could be dug out of the ground and smelted into immediately useable metal. No extensive trade network was required to bring component metals together. This became necessary in the post-apocalyptic period as trade withered. The Hittites were early miners and workers of the metal. Their position at the geographic nexus of both land and sea trade hastened the transfer of technology that brought the Iron Age, leading over centuries to the eventual development of the steel that supports modern civilization.

The last days of the Mycenaean Empire became the foundation of Western literature as the *Iliad* and the *Odyssey*. The plot lines and story-telling techniques are replicated endlessly in today's works of fiction.

The surviving cities of the fractured imperial confederation carried on. Within these incubated the earliest concept of democracy, as did the concept of science as a search for natural rather than supernatural causes for events.

These and other developments from Greek city-states infuse modern culture. Euclidean geometry is taught in high school. Colleges offer full term courses in the various philosophies developed in the Greek city-states. Theater groups perform the tragedies and comedies of Greek playwrights. Today's doctors take the oath of Hippocrates, who is credited with being the father of modern medicine. A charred and battered prayer book written over the scrubbed out writings of Archimedes fetched over two million dollars at auction. More millions were spent imaging his musings on higher mathematics.

The nation of Egypt today has much the same geographic boundaries as it did following the Hyksos Expulsion of the 16th Century BC. Intervening conquests have changed the social and religious dynamic. The Empire is gone. The old land of Canaan remains a battlefield, split now into the tortured states of Syria, Lebanon, Israel and Palestine. Since the imperial apocalypse it has been the birth place of Christianity and the site of the Crusades. From the land that was once the flashpoint of Egyptian and Hittite ambitions has grown the western religious heritage.

Egypt itself, by contrast, remained a stable refuge for keen intellects of the post apocalyptic period, a position enhanced following the conquests of Alexander the Great. The Library at Alexandria was, for centuries, the premier repository of written knowledge in the ancient world. Ptolemaic astronomy kept alive the study and measurement of the heavens. The writings of Hero(n) of Alexandria, a mathematician and engineer who developed among other things a coin operated vending machine and a mechanical door opener, survive from Arabic copies. The orthogonal layout of modern cities that we take for granted today, a grid of streets intersecting at right angles, was originated by the Egyptians.

The failure of the great empires of the Late Bronze Age did not plunge the Eastern Mediterranean into an abyss. Life went on for the survivors. Farmers farmed. Traders traded. The Biblical kings David and Solomon ruled during this period. Scripture describes their kingdoms in detail. The authors wax eloquent about the opulence of Solomon's court, but in terms of geographic area he controlled a relatively small principality. This situation was replicated across the Eastern Mediterranean. The social order that once held diverse elements together was gone. Urban centers lay ruined or abandoned. Resources grew scarce. Markets dried up. Commerce shrank to a fraction of imperial heights. The elements of post apocalyptic society had to be self-reliant.

Much of the contemporary writing from the Late Bronze Age comes to us from imperial archives. Without empires there were no more vast archives. Nor was there monumental architecture upon which achievements could be inscribed. In this sense the period was a dark age because it left no readily accessible or comprehensive record of activities. That is not to suggest there isn't much to be found. It is likely that literacy spread more widely during this period. Tantalizing fragments of carved letters have emerged from the desert. Shards of pottery contain evidence that writing was not uncommon. There may well be a trove of the documents of daily life such as those from Pylos and Ugarit awaiting discovery.

Until archaeology can pry loose the artifacts of the period and emerging science can better measure and interpret them, we are left with the contemporary accounts of the Egyptians and Assyrians, who witnessed events from some distance, and with later writing based on the oral tradition and lost documents to tell us what the Eastern Mediterranean looked like in the wake of the collapse.

The information we have presents a picture of small kingdoms and squabbling religious sects. Culture was often local and tribal. Both the Egyptians and the Assyrians mounted large scale raids, but neither was able to impose dominance or order in any but their own territory. In time, both saw their own power fade. The Phoenicians rose, but largely as traders rather than rulers. By the time the Persians tried their hand at conquest, the Greek city-states had grown too strong to be overcome.

It was more than eight hundred years after the imperial collapse of the Late Bronze Age that Alexander the Great left Macedonia on what would become his conquest of not only the Eastern Mediterranean but lands as far as India and Afghanistan. Civilization, at least as defined by the presence of a uniform social order, had returned. Its form was different and far better documented than the Late Bronze Age imperial period, although its life span was no greater. Roman legions were in control before the birth of Christ. One empire had given way to another.

It was some seven hundred years from the death of Sargon of Akkad to the rise of the Egyptian, Hittite and Mycenaean Empires, and more than eight hundred years until the time of Alexander the Great. These time spans speak to the difficulty of forging an empire in the formative years of the concept, and testify to the skill and vision of those who built Late Bronze Age society in the Eastern Mediterranean.

We have learned a great deal about the Late Bronze Age in the Eastern Mediterranean during the last two hundred years. Much of what we have come to know simply tells us how much more we have to discover. We are still not able to read any of the considerable finds of Minoan Linear A. Much of the other scripts we do know how to read goes either untransliterated or uninterpreted due to lack of resources.

Surprises emerge on a regular basis. Recent re-examination of several cuneiform tablets established that the Bronze Age Babylonians used geometric representation of the area under a curve to track the Planet Jupiter. This is a key concept of integral calculus, which modern history tells us was developed by Sir Isaac Newton in the 17th Century AD. Newton said that he was able to accomplish what he did because he stood on the shoulders of giants. This had led scholars to wonder what writing he may have had available to him that is lost now.

The Late Bronze Age was a time of giants. Not in any physical sense, but in the breadth of their knowledge, the scale of their daring and the scope of their achievements. Their civilization may have fallen, but it left as its legacy the foundations of the modern world.

ADDITIONAL READING

⌘

ANY BROAD HISTORY IS NECESSARILY an overview. Details for this work were selected to focus on two core questions; what we know and how we know it. Biographical information on the players was reduced to the minimum required to follow the narrative. The web of competing theories surrounding events was summarized. Fascinating tidbits of information, irrelevant beyond their ability to provide a flavor of the times, were omitted. For those interested in exploring the subject in more depth, the following reading list is offered.

Breasted, James Henry. 1903. *A History Of Egypt.* Charles Scribner's Sons.

Casson, Lionel. 1959. *The Ancient Mariners.* The MacMillan Company.

Ceram, C. W. (Kurt Merak). 1955. *The Secret of the Hittites.* Alfred A. Knopf.

Cline, Eric H. 2014. *1177 B.C.; The Year Civilization Collapsed.* Princeton University Press.

Drews, Robert. 1993. *The End of the Bronze Age.* Princeton University Press.

Fagles, Robert. 1998. *Translation of Homer's Iliad.* Penguin Publishing Group

Fagles, Robert. 1997. *Translation of Homer's Odyssey.* Penguin Publishing Group

Gray, John. 1962. *Archaeology and the Old Testament World.* Thomas Nelson and Sons Ltd.

Kerrigan, Michael. 2009. *The Ancients in Their Own Words.* Amber Books Ltd.

Lattimore, Richmond. 1953. *Translation of Aeschylus' Oresteia.* University of Chicago Press.

Macqueen, J.G. 1986. *The Hittites and their Contemporaries in Asia Minor.* Thames and Hudson Ltd.

Race, William H. 1959. *Translation of Apollonius of Rhodes' Voyage of Argo.* Penguin Classics.

Spalinger, Anthony J. 2005. *War in Ancient Egypt.* Blackwell Publishing

Ward, W. A. and Joukowsky, M. S. (Editors). 1992. *The Crisis Years: The 12th Century BC.* Kendall/Hunt Publishing Co.

Wood, Michael. 1985. *In Search of the Trojan War.* New American Library.

Woolly, C. Leonard. 1965. *The Sumerians.* Oxford University Press.